Struggling with Sex

A Serious
Call to
Marriage-Centered
Sexual Life

ARTHUR A. ROUNER JR.

AUGSBURG Publishing House • Min

STRUGGLING WITH SEX
A Serious Call to Marriage-Centered Sexual Life

Copyright © 1987 Augsburg Publishing House

Scripture quotations unless otherwise noted are from the Holy Bible: New International Version. Copyright 1978 by the New York International Bible Society. Used by permission of Zondervan Bible Publishers.

First names only are used with most of the stories told in this book. Unless otherwise noted, these names are fictitious and the specific details of the stories have been altered so as to make the characters unrecognizable.

Library of Congress Cataloging-in-Publication Data

Rouner, Arthur Acy Jr.
  STRUGGLING WITH SEX.

  1. Sex—Religious aspects—Christianity.
2. Marriage—Religious aspects—Christianity.
I. Title. [DNLM: 1. Marriage—popular works. 2. Morals—popular works. 3. Religion and Sex—popular works.
4. Sex Behavior—popular works. HQ 503 R859s]
BT708.R65 1986   241'.66   86-32028
ISBN 0-8066-2243-1

Manufactured in the U.S.A.   APH 10-6096

1 2 3 4 5 6 7 8 9 0 1 2 3 4 5 6 7 8 9

Contents

Preface

On a May Saturday I sat on the greensward of a northern Minnesota church camp. It was a beautiful, early spring afternoon on one of our state's 10,000 magnificent lakes. It was the ninth-grade confirmation retreat. It was hours before final "decision time," when 78 15-year-olds would be asked to look again at their own lives to see if they were ready to heed the call to commit to Jesus.

I was attempting to have a personal visit, right there on the grass, with some 25 of them—the ones who hadn't made it to my study in the previous weeks. I am their teacher and their minister. I love them and want to help them, though they don't all know that.

They come, one at a time, and sit down cross-legged on the grass, some more hesitant and nervous than others. One little girl, a tender heart who had occasionally hung back after class for a fleeting personal moment, began to talk about how the others looked down on her. I asked why. "Because they know I've asked for help on tests sometimes. They think I'm a bad girl."

Suddenly, with almost no transition, she was looking right at me and talking about being sexually abused.

"Your father?" I asked, incredulously, for he was a sweet-spirited man of the flock who seemed both ingenuous and sincerely committed.

"No, my brother," she said. Then quickly she corrected it all, saying, "Well, not abuse. It was mutual. We did it for a couple of years. I love my brother. He is the only one who really understands me. I feel terrible, but I love him. We don't do it anymore, and he's gone off to college. I don't know why God let it all happen."

A confused view of God was strangely mixed with a horror story of incest, and yet of love and longing, prompted in part, at least, by a demeaned view of herself. And within 10 minutes, sitting in that summer camp setting of innocence and nostalgia, this tender, wounded child had laid it right out on the grass for her minister–teacher to see.

I was shocked and dismayed by the particularity of it, and by the depth of it. But it was merely confirmation of what we knew was going on among dozens and scores, if not hundreds, of our church youngsters—and if among them, how much more among their contemporaries.

A man in his 50s, once a church leader, often seeks me out for lunch. I care for him deeply. He tells me about his life and work. Usually he confesses the latest episodes in his running battle with himself over his sexual passions. I know of his affair within his company with a married woman. I know he loves his wife and wants to stay with her. I know he feels helpless to resist the pull of the other relationship. It is dangerous professionally, and it is suicidal for his marriage. Each time we meet he asks my prayers for him in his lonely, private battle.

On some days it seems the whole world is struggling

with sex. Perhaps it is only the Christians, but at least they struggle, whether it is the 15-year-old or the 50-year-old. American society is struggling with its sexuality. Parents increasingly feel caught in a dilemma, trying to offer a standard to teenage children. Congressmen have their struggles with sex, involving sometimes the house pages, both male and female. A judge was discovered to be having illicit sexual relations after court when the robes of dispassion and judicial wisdom were off. No less are priests and ministers free of the struggle. In the age group 15 to 17, one of every two boys and one of every three girls in this country has had sexual intercourse.

Something has happened to us as a society. Sexual experience, licit and illicit, is open to all. Many people justify it, and, in some cases, encourage it.

If such a life-style of sexual relationships with anyone were making all of us happy and fulfilled, then maybe ministers, counselors, and teachers would have to say, "They seem to have something. They're all so whole and happy and fulfilled."

But the opposite is true. The baby boom generation—and many of those who have been influenced by it—is not happy, not fulfilled. In many ways, these people are miserable.

Who will help them? It seems audacious to step forward and offer another book on sex to help with the struggle. But I do offer it, because there is a way of looking at the struggle that to my knowledge has not been articulated. I believe it needs to be, and that it can help. Please accept this book as a point of view that could change—dramatically for the better—your understanding, and maybe your living out, of the sexual struggle you face. It is sent out to help as many people as possible with this big and private and personal human dilemma.

ONE

The Meaning of Morality

Something new is happening in America in relation to sex. More and more people want it to mean something. They're tired of having sex be something you do with just any old body. They want it to be "special" again. They want it to be unique, something different from anything else they do. They want it to stand for a relationship that is personal and important and unlike any other relationship they experience.

Every year two or three couples, discussing in my study their plans to be married, have said, "Oh, we partied and played around and had sex with a number of people. But when we met each other, we realized the sex we had enjoyed before had had no meaning. It was just mechanical. We want it to mean more to us in our new relationship in marriage, so we decided early on in our relationship not to have sexual intercourse with each other. It's hard, but we feel it's important for our future marriage."

These are not people who were brought up to have a strong belief about sexual abstinence before marriage. They freely confess to having "played around" and used a number of partners. But when they came together in love for each other, there seemed to be a new factor involved.

For one thing, they were usually young people who had found a new faith, a love for Jesus that they hadn't known before. That faith made all relationships more important to them.

Along with that, they found that they wanted their personal relationship with each other, this new thing, this marriage into which they were about to enter, to have a deeper meaning than any of the other relationships they had had.

They decided that the way they had "done sex" before— not only without love, but without commitment—had taken meaning away from the act of sexual intercourse. That act had signified nothing, and they now wanted it to signify something. They wanted it to be a sign of their committed, permanent relationship.

The only way they could think of to restore that meaning was by not having sex at all. By denying that pleasure to themselves now, they realize that the act will have more meaning for them later when they enter into it as husband and wife.

They had discovered that what they had been doing before, the way they had been using the act of sexual intercourse, was "wrong." It did not honor a human relationship. It had not lifted up or helped a "right" relationship. It had been "immoral," inasmuch as it was an act performed out of an uncommitted relationship. What they found themselves longing for was a "right" relationship, one that was therefore "moral."

They had learned that lesson practically, out of their personal experience. The old way, they realized, hadn't made them happy, and it had seemed to make quite mechanical and meaningless an act that they had supposed should be an act of great intimacy and tenderness.

Every one of the 30 or so couples who come to me each year to be married wants the same thing. All of them want a lifetime together, of intimacy, of deeply shared human experience with someone they care about very much.

But most of them have not connected that goal, that deep desire in their minds, with the way they are using, or abusing, their sexuality. They all want the end result, the high goal of an intimate life with another, but they are not sure how to get it. Something, they are beginning to suspect, has been missing. Lots of people are discovering that something has been missing in what "everybody thinks" about sex, and about what's right and wrong in sex.

Many parents are having second thoughts these days about sexuality. One of them is the syndicated writer, Ellen Goodman:*

I belong to a whole generation of people who grew up under traditional rules about sex. We heard all about the rights and wrongs, shoulds and shouldn'ts, dos and don'ts.

As adults, we have lived through a time when all these rules were questioned, when people were set "free" to discover their own sexuality, their own definitions of sexual values and morality. Whether we observed this change or were part of it, we were affected by it. Now, with all our ambivalence and confusion, we are the new crop of parents of growing children.

Our agenda is a complicated one, because we do not want to be the new guardians of sexual repression. Nor are we willing to define sexual freedom as the children's right to

---

*Quotations from Ellen Goodman are from her article, "The Turmoil of Teenage Sexuality: Parents' Mixed Signals," *Ms.*, July 1983. Used by permission of Ellen Goodman.

"do it." We are equally uncomfortable with notions that Sex is Evil and Sex is Groovy.

Parents of our generation want to talk to our children. We know that from one study after another. Yet we also know from the same research that, in fact, we are saying very little to our children about sex. In large part, our silence grows out of our own uneasiness and our uncertainties about sexuality in general, and the sexual "revolution" in particular. Many of us are still uneasy with our own evolving standards, are uncertain about the mixed results of the changing sexual mores. We feel conflict between protecting our children and freeing them.

As less traditional parents, we have an easier time than some of our peers when we offer sexual information. But we have a much harder time discussing morals. After all, our lessons for young people are not a rigid series of dos and don'ts, but a long list of whens and under-what-conditions.

A sex educator and parent in Washington, D.C., contemplating the murky goals of her two roles, asked the questions this way: "What should our task be? Should it be to prevent premarital sexual activity or to forestall it until something called an appropriate age? Should it be to prevent sexual activity or merely conception? Or should it be to encourage sex as joyful, with a loving, contraceptively protected partner?"

Another woman with a 13-year-old daughter, who studied the parents of adolescents, says, "We're trying to communicate a situational norm, like, it's okay under certain circumstances. If you both honest-to-god want to. If you think you'll be in each other's lives for a while. If you are responsible. If you use birth control, if you are old enough, if you won't get hurt, if you have a wholesome sexual experience." Her list of "ifs" extends into the air.

"In the face of such confusion," says Dr. Greer Litton Fox, who also studied parental messages at Wayne State

University, "it should not be surprising that many parents have sidestepped the matter entirely."

Not only have parents avoided discussing sexual values with teenagers, but many adults have no clear view, even for ourselves, of what sexuality is all about and what it is really for. Practiced with the abandon and indiscrimination of the last two decades, sexuality has not led to universal happiness.

Goodman quotes Ruth MacDonald, who has directed a parent-education program in Newton, Massachusetts:

I think teenage sex is usually a fairly minimal experience in many ways. The girl is usually scared to death. She doesn't want her parents to think she's a bad girl. She's still very involved with her parents while she's doing it with a boy. He's very worried about performance and liking her, but not wanting to get stuck forever. Most of it happens with a lot of their clothes on.

I've been all over the country talking to girls in schools for teenage parents especially. The girls getting pregnant aren't having a hell of a good time.

Most of us, whatever our age, long for sexual fulfillment, but we despair of finding it, even with those we love most dearly and have lived with, and even when we have worked on it for years.

Getting married does not end the agony. The experiments before marriage do not dissipate or rule out sexual struggle after marriage. A cauldron of feelings, passions, conflicts, unspoken agendas, and deep longings seems to seethe in the soul of all of us, all through life, but we can help each other by acknowledging the unspoken plea of Ellen Goodman to offer up some hints about values, about meaning, and, therefore, about morality.

A Search for Order

The significance of morals is not in their restrictions and limitations, which is the way most of us tend to think of them. Their significance is in the order they offer, the guidance they give, and the means of measuring our life and finding our way, particularly in finding our way into a sense of rightness about what we are doing, a sense that what we are doing is good, fair, and fulfilling. People, after all, do have consciences. They do care about what is right and wrong.

One young businesswoman in her mid-20s was going through divorce and came to our church. One Sunday she approached me after the service, asking if she could come see me. We met for coffee one night at a local restaurant. The saddest of tales poured out.

"My divorce is final. I haven't been with my husband for months. Now I'm pregnant by a man I barely know. For years in my marriage I wanted to get pregnant and have a child, but my husband wouldn't hear of it. Now that I'm divorced, I'm pregnant by a man I don't love and wouldn't marry anyway.

"I don't know whether to have an abortion or not. I have a good job and travel extensively for my company. I'm embarrassed to be pregnant. They all know I'm no longer married.

"I know if I have this child I'll want to keep it, but I'm not sure I have either the emotional strength to care for a child or the ability to juggle my work and be a mom and manage in any way to support myself. What shall I do?"

Far from being insensitive and uncaring and simply wanting to use abortion as a means of birth control, she was all sensitivity and compassion.

From my limited experience I tried to suggest what I knew about the trauma and aftereffects of the abortion experience.

"I know," she said. "I've already had one abortion before my marriage." She knew all about it. She didn't need any bad news from me.

We looked at the alternatives, particularly the possibility of carrying the baby full term and then giving it up for adoption. There were more tears, and no real resolution. We prayed and parted.

Two weeks later she thrust a note into my hand after church. I have read it many times since.

Dear Arthur,

Somehow with such hectic schedules it seems easier to leave a note for you than to make phone contact.

Shortly after we met I made the decision to carry the child full term. The actual act of "making the decision" to do this is not so difficult as is living it.

I am of the opinion a child is a miracle of Christ. It should be a cheerful, celebrated occasion. If I keep the child, I am blessed with that creation. If I give the child up for adoption to a family who desires the child, they will have that joy. Either way, there are many things to be grateful for and happy about. Now that is how I feel when I sit quietly and really look at what counts in life. In the day-to-day rush of life it is far more difficult to keep a positive outlook on the situation.

Certainly there are many problems to be dealt with. Somehow the people in the world are so busy with the problems and worries that the joy is lost. I will not survive seven months without joy—and with exaggerated concerns.

I don't want this child to ever feel it's an inconvenience or a burden, because truly the inconveniences are minor.

And so I ask you to remember my thoughts and needs in your prayers—that day to day my spirits stay up, looking for the glory in each day.

Thank you so much for the love and support you have given me. I appreciate it so.

Thank you so, so much.

How much she cares! How real is her agony! I did not moralize with her about the adulterous sexual relationship that got her in trouble in the first place. That was already all too clear to her. Our job was to find a way out of the dilemma into which she had trapped herself.

She found a way, a difficult way, but an honorable one that made her feel right about what she was doing. Through it all it gave her a sense of being a moral person who did care, someone with standards and principles.

The struggle underneath was with this strange power within called sex. She had been unclear about the right or wrong of it. Who knows how she fell into the second affair. She only knew that it left her wretched and lost. Her passion, her desire had led to a difficult human problem affecting two lives, her job, her future, and her mental health.

Finally she found a way to turn that passion and its unhappy consequences into a new channel that could bring some good in her life, and that could make her sin and sorrow and suffering into the means of a new joy and fulfillment, an expression of love in another human being. Somehow the whole situation came round to at least one of the ultimate purposes for which God gave us the sexual act and its joyful experience.

We appear to be coming to a new view of the meaning of morality in relation to our struggle with sex. My young friend came to it out of painful personal experience.

A Concern for Our Children

Others, like Ellen Goodman, are parents troubled by what their own "new morality" has wrought. They may not recognize what it has done in their own lives, but they readily see what it is doing in the lives of their children.

These parents had rebelled against the restrictions of what they view as "traditional morality." They fear what they felt was its legalism, its self-righteousness, its unbending uncharity. But, like Ms. Goodman, they have come to fear, as well, the opposite extreme, and the glib cheapness of the view that sex is just one more thing you do for amusement. They are a generation in their 30s and 40s who have begun to fear the shallowness of what liberated sex has become—especially as they see the hurt that view appears now to be inflicting on the lives of their children, that next generation of wonderful but drifting teenagers.

For these parents the dilemma is not yet resolved. Many are troubled in their own lives. Many find their marriages failing, and they are not quite sure why. It hurts them to see their children hurt, but many of them are so hurt themselves they are unable to see the need of their child, or to help even if they see the need.

An increasing number of them are people suffering the grief of divorce. They have been rejected by someone they loved and trusted. They have been through bitter court battles. In some cases friends have turned against them. Many of them are now single mothers attempting to fulfill the "mission impossible" of being super moms, trying to succeed as competent businesswomen in the world and as mothers to children at the same time.

They have been hurt by men. They are full of anger, and some of that is transmitted to their children. Those children of divorce themselves feel abandoned, so they, too, are angry.

The ninth-grade youngsters whom I teach in their confirmation year have been living examples of all these tensions. In any recent year nearly half of them are the children of divorced parents. Sometimes they don't know who they are or whose they are. They are angry at their parents for divorcing each other and abandoning them, and they are angry at themselves because of the unspoken fear that they themselves somehow caused the divorce.

Their divorced parents do not really know "what's right." In their divorce, they have done what they never dreamed they would do, and they wonder if some sort of free sex might even now be better. If they have held to an old morality, they feel that morality has betrayed them.

One divorced and remarried mother of a 15-year-old girl who had just finished ninth grade made it clear that she believed her daughter should have the right to make choices—as a teenager—about sexual involvement with boys, and she is providing her with means of birth control. Perhaps only when she sees for herself the confusions and hurts all those disordered and uncommitted intimate relationships will wreak upon her daughter will she begin to search for some other way.

Such sexual activity on the part of teenage children may seem acceptable to some parents, but when they recognize the destructive and complicating options facing their children in drug and alcohol use at appallingly young ages, mixed with apparently endless sexual opportunities, many parents are looking for help. They are beginning to ask if those enlightened, liberal views of sexuality and sexual practice really make much sense after all.

The suddenly awakening concern about values arises primarily out of a concern for society's children. It is one thing to accept freedom and license in sexual matters for ourselves, but it is quite something else to observe what is beginning to happen to our children. After all, we feel rather differently about our own offspring—"bone of my bones, and flesh of my flesh," as the Bible says. These people are our own, part of ourselves, and they are precious to us. They are our own future, and in many ways they are our hope. Now we see them as vulnerable. We see them hurt in deep and sometimes permanent ways by their relationships. The implications of their mistakes and misjudgments are suddenly quite permanent. They must live with them for many years.

We discover that it is now our children, 15–26 years old, who are the loneliest segment of the population—more lonely than the widowed and even abandoned people of old age—and the nation's highest suicide rate is among these youngsters.

What we're seeing is that we have allowed or encouraged our young people to take on experiences and responsibilities that we ourselves can scarcely handle in middle age. We begin to see we may have stuck our children with relationships and responsibilities they in no way can handle, and we're beginning to feel badly about it—in fact, guilty about it. We feel guilty that, as parents, we have done so little to prepare our children with sexual knowledge for this strange, new world. We have been as inept and unskilled and frightened and embarrassed as any generation before us in saying anything of significance to our children about sex.

As a counselor to hundreds of young couples coming to be married and to many others disillusioned and wanting to get out of their marriages, I thought I had commented and conversed and philosophized about love and marriage and sexual issues to my own five children, either in their presence or directly to them at the family dinner table, over lingering breakfast coffee on our summertime vacations, and on long travels in the family van. Yet the most modern and aware of my three daughters, who graduated from an excellent women's college preparing young women especially for careers in fashion, art, and the media, exploded one day, saying to both her mother and me: "You never told me anything about sex—none of the real particulars!" We had said lots about the meaning, but little about the specifics, the practicalities, the acts of love, and the precautions of responsibility.

One journal says, "Parents want their children to have rich, loving, sexual lives, but they don't want them to make babies."

"Our conditional approval of sex," says Ellen Goodman, "is the product of our best hopes and also of our reservations about the sexual revolution. The changes in our adulthood and our children's lives have not been all sweet. The fallout can be measured, is regularly measured, in the front-page statistics about an 'epidemic' of teenage pregnancies, venereal disease and abortions. They are also measured in the softer evidence of our children's—especially our daughters'—vulnerabilities."

Goodman is probing at and groping toward values in sexuality—the meaning of it all. She fears to give up the sense of freedom and personal choice for children, but she is painfully aware of the hurt that seems almost inevitable for children experiencing, long before their time, the deep feelings and struggles of adult sexuality.

"The reality," Goodman says, "is that for all our difficulty in communicating values to our kids, they learn anyway. They learn from our own reactions and relationships. Our kids hear us talking to each other, reacting to what's in the news or local gossip or advertising. They eavesdrop on our lives. More of them now, especially the children of single parents, deal with us as sexual beings than ever before.

"It is easier to be comfortable with our children's sexuality if we are comfortable with our own. . . . and that's no mean feat. To set up a dialogue at adolescence, we have to be willing to offer up our views, our anxieties, our angers."

Her admission is the one we all must make if we are to be honest: we are confused. We are not sure about this sexual revolution. We are not sure we like what it is doing to our children or to us. We are not sure we like what it is doing to dozens of our friends and their marriages. We feel a great loss, if not of innocence, perhaps of meaning, of depth, of integrity, of wholeness.

Looking for a New Way

It is morality we look for—a new sense of a right and wrong, a way to be whole and integrated and ordered in our lives, a new way, "to feel good about ourselves," about who we are and what we stand for. We long to have all the aspects of our lives integrated and connected. The vague sense of guilt, either about ourselves or about our children, we long to have forgiven. The "new morality" that said, "Do what seems good, what won't hurt anybody, what meets the particular situation, and is the loving thing," just hasn't been enough.

Where is there such a standard? Who can tell our children 16 is too young for sexual intercourse, and 17 or 18 is old enough? What makes the later age more responsible, better able to avoid the agonies of deep feelings and conflicts that go along with sexual intercourse and the intimacy it implies?

Maybe it has nothing to do with age. In a society where young people of 25 and 30 do not feel ready yet to marry, what makes sexual intercourse for unmarried late teenagers with no job, no home of their own, and no recognized public relationship somehow OK?

Morality means a view of life that, if put into practice and lived out, contributes to wholeness and health, to meaning and joy. Its common acceptance makes the life of the community possible. It allows people to trust each other, to have expectations of each other, to function together as a society.

I believe there is such a way to understand our sexuality and to order it and use it and rejoice in it. The signs out there in the land, and in much of my own counseling and pastoral experience with hundreds of people, indicate that this modern world we live in is feeling a new willingness to look again at what it means to be sexual beings with passionate feelings that need to be understood and ordered. It is these possibilities that I am eager to explore in the chapters that follow.

TWO

The Bottom Line in Sex: Marriage

Marriage has never been a more booming business than it is today. Everybody's doing it. They may have done it before. It may even have turned out to be the most painful human relationship they have ever experienced. But they always seem game to try it again.

Something about that strange institution still draws people into it. Whether it is the desire to have someone to depend on, or a longing for intimacy, or the attraction of Robert Browning's wistful invitation to "come, grow old with me," there seems to be no decrease in the number of people who want to "tie themselves down" to another human being in a permanent, lifetime relationship of commitment.

The curious thing is that this is true in a period in American life when young people are marrying later and when most of them no longer feel they have to be married in order to enjoy sexual intercourse. Given that assumption, I wonder why they bother to marry at all. It would seem much more logical to simply live on together, allowing the relationship to become common-law marriage if they wanted it. But to go through all the preparations for a wedding, and to employ all the symbols of fresh, new beginnings, such as the white bridal dress for virginity when virginity is something most of them lost long ago, seems a pointless exercise. Besides, a wedding for 150-300 people costs more than it ever did.

Why do they do it? Clearly, they want to be bound, to be united to another. They want to be in a relationship from which they can't easily get out. They do want to "grow old together." They all say it.

But they haven't connected in their minds the act of sexual intercourse with marriage. They had believed the assumption that our society was making in the '60s and '70s, that the sexual experience is for everybody, a natural human right like the right to life, liberty, and the pursuit of happiness, or the right to vote, or the right to live wherever you'd like or can afford to live.

While parents may not want to know about it or see it, many assume that their unmarried children are having some sort of sexual experience. Statistics show us that high school students are engaging in sexual intercourse in fairly large numbers, and life in a college dormitory in the '70s and '80s has often included bunking in with friends every once in a while so your roommate could have that special friend of the opposite sex in for an "overnight."

The live-in relationships before marriage that have become so common in the last decade were nearly unheard of in the college generation of their parents in the early '50s, but parents have been loathe to protest this movement and have felt constrained from imposing their moral views on their children. Meanwhile, the television jokes about marriage relationships, divorce, and alimony, coupled with the hedonistic philosophy of Hugh Hefner and the highly erotic undertone of American advertising, have created a climate of wide acceptance of varied sexual relationships and experimentation. They have subtly but swiftly changed the basic assumptions about sexuality not only of the young, but of the middle-aged as well. But even in the midst of this dramatic change in attitude, there still lurks a longing for permanence and loyalty and trust in marriage.

Many wonderful young people come to the church to be married. Because of our commitment to Christian marriage, or at least the marriage of people who are trying to work out a living faith in their marriage, we require several counseling sessions for anyone being married in the church by one of our ministers: two sessions with the minister who is going to perform the ceremony, a session with the counseling minister to discuss a compatibility test that all couples take, as well as a session with a lay couple trained by the church to give another perspective on the marriage experience. A fifth meeting with a member of our Wedding Committee, trained to help with the many physical details of the rehearsal and wedding itself, means that each couple has met with several people of the church family before their wedding, and we know each other pretty well.

It is our privilege to do it, but we require it because we believe we are fighting on a critical battlefront for the survival of marriage, especially the kind of marriage about which we care, and which we think most people unconsciously yearn to have for themselves.

The trouble is that they don't know how to create this marriage. They don't know how to build it. They don't know what it takes. They don't understand how those foundations are laid. They don't even realize that the way they live before marriage, the assumptions they make about sex, and what they do sexually has everything to do with either building sure foundations for their marriage or with planting a time bomb in that marriage even before it has begun.

Sex surely is not everything in marriage, but it is an important part. It is the deep, physical expression of that intimate bond of love that draws two people together in marriage and then holds them and deepens and binds them in a relationship of intimacy and permanence.

What has been lost is any awareness that sexual expression, at least at the level of the intimacy of intercourse, is the unique act of marriage. It is the privilege of marriage and the expression of married love.

Most of the people who come to us in the church to prepare for marriage don't know that. It hasn't occurred to them. Marriage, they think, is about love. And "nobody ever had such a love as ours," is invariably the message they convey to me. "We are going to make it in marriage, because we're so wonderful," is what they're actually saying.

Beyond Communication

They tell me how well they communicate. "We can say anything to each other," they report. "We always say what we think." "I love Suzy because she helps me get it out and not stuff any angry feelings. We're going to make it because we communicate so well." It is their skills in communication that they look to to be the strength and rock of their marriage.

We've become a highly psychologized society. We know all the jargon. We've been told to "let it all hang out," that "I'm OK, you're OK." That we should "do whatever feels good," that we should "be good to yourself," "put yourself first." In a pop sort of way we know all about getting our feelings out, and about how important good communication is.

But do we really communicate that well? Why are we such an increasingly angry society? How come we're all so mad at each other? Why is every other marriage in America breaking up? Why are many that haven't ended in divorce unhappy and often silent standoffs? From where will reconciliation come? How will forgiveness be learned? Is good communication all there is?

Georgiana and Mike came to see me to prepare for their marriage. Georgiana had joined the church that spring and seemed to think I was a good fellow and our church a good place. Mike, on the other hand, I had never seen before. He was several years younger than Georgiana. They both came from rural backgrounds, and in our first interview they talked at length about the solidity of their moral values, in contrast to big-city ideas of the fast track. Mike spoke of how Georgiana was a homebody type and wasn't always on the go, and how much he liked coming home to her and just sitting at home and being quiet together.

As they went on, it was only too apparent that they were already living together. I asked them about that. They had been living together for three years. Though I usually don't discuss sexual issues on my first meeting with couples, I took a chance and asked Mike and Georgiana how they felt living together in a sexual relationship for three years before marriage squared with the conservative "rural values" that they had seemed to espouse? How did the folks down on the farm feel about that kind of life-style as a preparation for marriage?

From that moment on it was clear that in their view I had overstepped the bounds of pastoral privilege. (I normally have used the first visit to gain couples' trust by learning about their lives and work and why they love each other and what they have found in common.) Georgiana's face reddened, her eyes grew big with dismay, and then began to fill with tears. She leaped to her feet and left the room. When she returned, she was still shocked that I could think they were anything but the most moral of people. Why, they had long since committed themselves to each other, and as far as they were concerned, they were just as married as they would be after the ceremony.

"Why, then, have the ceremony?" I asked.

"Well! We want to have God's blessing, and we want to do it for our family's sake."

"But you are asking God to bless something he has specifically commanded us not to do in his commandment against adultery. You've changed the rules. You're expecting God to bless and go along with what you have determined is right, rather than you going along with what he asks and has specifically stated he expects of you."

They could not see it. She was deeply hurt that I had a view of sex and marriage different from theirs, one that included different assumptions from theirs. They had made their view up themselves, or they had accepted it from the world around them, and taken it as the norm— which indeed, it has become in our society. They continued to think of themselves as moral and faithful Christian people. I was the one who had overstepped, who had demeaned them by presuming to suggest that the morality they had created as a basis for their marriage was not the biblical view.

Like many people, Mike and Georgiana didn't have much acquaintance with the biblical view. They were not literate in the Bible. They knew their parents didn't approve of their life-style, but the prevailing world view around them was much more to their liking and fit more nearly with what they wanted to do—which was to have sex together, to do whatever came "naturally."

They were good and decent people. They hadn't cheated others, robbed banks, or anything of the kind, but they had a poor foundation for their marriage, according to the best biblical insights.

Like most of the couples who come to us, Mike and Georgiana had written their own ticket. They had embraced a view that as long as they loved Jesus with their mind and heart they could do anything they wanted with their bodies. It was a separation of faith from ethics, and it is, in my view, a prescription for disaster in marriage, because it fails to honor the power and importance of sexual intercourse to stand as the symbol and unique act of a relationship that is much more than pleasure and even more than love. This relationship is based on commitment, in which two people pledge their lives, their hearts and bodies, to each other forever. This relationship is perfectly enacted by the tender, intimate act of sexual intercourse, which the Bible, in the creation account, and later in the words of Jesus, points to as the special act of two people of the opposite sex who are married. What has happened in America in the past 20 years is that this biblical view has been lost.

The Lost Biblical View

The Bible is a book of love. Its Old Testament is earthy, honest, and candid about sexual passion and the human need for it. The New Testament is spendthrift with love and rejoices with forgiveness—even and especially toward the woman caught in the act of adultery, whom the priests were so ready to condemn. Jesus made Mary Magdalene, probably once a prostitute, his confidante and friend. He did not see divorce as putting one beyond the pale of God's love. He acknowledged that it is sin—a separating and breaking act—but never suggested it is beyond forgiveness.

He implied the same about adultery—that it too is sin, but it does not put one beyond the reach of God's love and forgiveness.

Some Pharisees once asked Jesus, "Is it lawful for a man to divorce his wife for any and every reason?" (Matt. 19:3).

Jesus asked them, "Haven't you read that at the beginning the Creator 'made them male and female,' and said, 'For this reason a man will leave his father and mother and be united to his wife, and the two will become one flesh'? So they are no longer two, but one. Therefore what God has joined together, let man not separate" (Matt. 19:4-6).

"Why then," they asked, "did Moses command that a man give his wife a certificate of divorce and send her away?"

Jesus replied, "Moses permitted you to divorce your wives because your hearts were hard. But it was not this way from the beginning. I tell you that anyone who divorces his wife, except for marital unfaithfulness, and marries another woman commits adultery" (Matt. 19:8-9).

Jesus did not overrule Moses. Jesus allowed for divorce, but he said it has consequences: it makes for adultery. Breaking one relationship (which God has joined together) and taking up another compromises, makes impure, sullies, and makes broken and wretched the first relationship.

Jesus called the proverbial spade a spade. He said you do damage in both divorce and adultery. You hurt people. You break relationships. Indeed, you break your relationships with God, which is why adultery is forbidden in the Ten Commandments. It fractures human bonds and divine bonds, and it creates immeasurable human pain.

Is that not true? Is it not the most honest thing that can be said about the delicate, intimate, human relationship of marriage, and all that threatens it?

Jesus' own example was his forgiveness of the woman caught in the act of adultery. Adultery itself—painful, guilty act that it is—is not the end of life. It is not beyond forgiveness and restoration, if the human heart is sorry, grieves for what it has done, and dares to turn around, repent, and seek forgiveness.

That is the joy and possibility of biblical faith about our agonizing human relationships and our awful compromises. They can be repaired. They do not have to be final. We do not have to be condemned. There is a way out. There is healing. There is mercy. The repairing of human relationships, the healing of hearts and hurts is what the Bible is about.

The Bible is about love and giving love a chance in human life. "I have come," Jesus said, "that they may have life, and have it to the full" (John 10:10). "My command is this: Love each other as I have loved you. Greater love has no one than this, that one lay down his life for his friends" (John 15:12-13). Here is complete, giving love—but with a standard, an order, a morality. It is not forbidding, not repressive or angry or cruel. It describes a way that lifts up human beings, honoring them for who they are, and loving them.

The Bible emphasizes mutuality and support for each other in the married relationship. The apostle Paul says that in marriage a husband and wife owe each other their bodies in a sexual way. The only reason, he suggests, for not having sexual intercourse with each other as married partners is by mutual agreement to abstain to "devote yourselves to prayer" (1 Cor. 7:5). In other words, sexual intercourse is viewed as a vital necessity for men and women in marriage. It is necessary and important for their growing life together. It is a gift given to them for joy, for mutual sharing, and pleasure in each other. It is for their health and wholeness.

The apostles saw the sexual relationship as something good and beautiful and fulfilling, something to make us happy, something to cause joy and delight and pleasure between a husband and wife.

The apostles apparently did not see sex simply as a means for procreation. It was a gift of joy and pleasure first, and only secondly a means to produce children as the happy overflow and outgrowth of that original committed relationship. The historic biblical view was more pro-sex and pro-pleasure than many 20th-century church people or their critics have understood.

The Meaning Is in Marriage

For the Bible, the key is marriage. And it is precisely marriage that has scared the freed-up sexual revolution people of recent decades.

Any view based on biblical principles sees sexual intercourse primarily as the act of two people in a marriage, not as an act of joy and pleasure for unmarried people. That, of course, has been the great complaint of modern American society. "Why can't sex be for everybody? Who says it's just for married people? In a world of more and more single people, including many divorced, why should sexual fulfillment be denied to perfectly decent, contributing members of society who happen not to be married?"

At one time we expected everyone to be married eventually, so sex before or outside of marriage was largely an issue of sex for the young, for teenagers, for those not yet ready for marriage. But this world of unmarried singles of all ages is different from what many of us expected.

And in our society, who wants to deny pleasure to anyone? Who wants to keep anyone else from having fun? So it seemed logical to create a social order in which sexual intimacy is offered to anyone. "Mutually consenting adults" was the phrase used to legitimize this view.

The pill set the stage for free and painless sex. Nobody had to worry anymore about getting pregnant (or, so we thought!). Then it was necessary to legitimize sex as pleasure for everyone, with no restraints. And that meant showing how the opposition, those who still restricted intercourse to marriage, were hypocritical, irrelevant, self-righteous, judgmental, rigid, unbending, and essentially unloving. Once the church and the nuclear family were depicted as insensitive and irrelevant, a new sexual philosophy could be created, based on advertising and popular psychology and philosophy.

This was done by Hugh Hefner and the *Playboy* philosophy, by talk show hosts with their offhand, late-night ridiculing of marriage and legitimizing of divorce and alimony, and by American advertising, which has used women to sell everything from whiskey ("Feel the Black Velvet") to cigarettes ("You've Come a Long Way, Baby") to clothes and cars.

Sex has been promoted as the province of everyone, even the right of everyone. This goes from the indiscriminate sexual encounters in the spirit of, "Well, you're gorgeous and I'm healthy, and we have a couple of hours between planes, so why not?" all the way to those who justify sexual intercourse "because we love each other."

In the minds of many people, sexual contact with anyone, for any reason, has been legitimized. It is viewed as what healthy, normal, attractive people do. While prostitution as paid-for sex is still often seen as demeaning and has the force of law working against it, the "sophisticated" assumption is that sex with any other consenting adult is OK.

On the other hand, countless others recoil from any such indiscriminate sexual contact as prostitution or a casual encounter with someone in the office or the neighborhood, but would feel completely justified in entering into sexual intercourse with someone they were in love with. "Love" has been the great justifying and legitimizing factor in spreading the sexual revolution to many people who would not, in an earlier day, have had any part in it. In the last two decades, "loving someone" or a "loving relationship" has made sexual intercourse acceptable. And this has been true with many people of faith who know all about the Ten Commandments and the warning against adultery. Love, they feel, makes it all OK.

The morality the Bible offers is a different basis for two people entering into a relationship of sexual intercourse. When Jesus quoted the creation story in Genesis and said that the way God meant it to be was for a man to "leave his father and mother and be united to his wife, and the two will become one flesh," he was identifying sexual intercourse as *the central, symbolic act* of marriage (Mark 10:7-8). He was not talking of two people being healthy and beautiful and attracted to each other, or even of two people being in love with each other. Instead, he suggested that becoming "one flesh," being "united," was in itself a powerful sign, a symbol, of a deep relationship between a man and a woman, of an agreed covenant with each other, a lifetime commitment we call marriage.

The Value of Commitment

In lifting up marriage, the Bible assumes love and mutual attraction. For the same reason the marriage service itself says little about love. It says a lot about duty, obligation, responsibility, and honor, because it is concerned with the establishment of a relationship—a permanent, lifetime commitment of two people with each other, which because of its permanence will offer the opportunity for growth, experimentation, forgiveness, healing, and maturing. In this way a relationship of depth and abiding trust and loyalty can be built as the foundation of a committed relationship that allows within it the right to "have a bad day" or "a bad year" and still be loved and supported by the partner.

To stay together "as long as it is a good relationship," to stay together "as long as we both shall love," is a profound threat to marriage. It says, "You'd better be good, you'd better be the way I like you, or I'll turn around and leave." That, in fact, is the unspoken basis for all live-in affairs: "I'll stay with you as long as you're OK, or you perform, or you're good—but if it gets bad, by whatever measure I may choose to apply, I'm getting out!" On such a basis trust is impossible. Loyalty is impossible. What the now-troubled generation of people in their 30s or 40s is struggling for is some basis for human relationship by which loyalty and trust are possible, so that the relationship is not simply two people using one another—either sexually or emotionally. The Bible asks, What relationship can offer any kind of moral, mutually supportive commitment of two people to each other apart from marriage?

In an affair, or even in a presumably permanent live-in relationship, many people say they are "committed," but when "push comes to shove," they are not committed. Either one of them is free to walk away from the other. Legally and morally, there is nothing to hold them.

There is only one context of commitment—and that is marriage. Only there has a promise been made that says, "I'll stay with you, stand by you, no matter what happens, no matter how you change, or the circumstances of our life change. 'For better, for worse, for richer, for poorer, in sickness and in health,' I am yours. This relationship is not fly-by-night. It is responsible. It says, "I love you, and I will be here in the morning. If a baby is conceived out of this act, I'll still be here to share my life with you and with that child. I am responsible to you. I am *one* with you."

What it is hard for society at large to see is that sexual intercourse, in its very act of two people coming together and literally entering into each other's bodies, is a symbol and sign of the unity, the uniting, the making one of those two people. It is, therefore, *the* sign, in all of human history—from the creation until now—of marriage. It is not a sign of love, nor a sign of sexual attraction, although it includes those two aspects of sexuality. It is a sign of that human relationship that comes about when two people in love enter into a permanent agreement of committed trust and loyalty to each other—under all circumstances.

In the view of biblical morality, sexual intercourse is tied inextricably to marriage. Marriage is the only relationship that offers the commitment that all of us long for with another human being.

To sort out our society's struggle and our personal struggle with sex, we need to take a new look at the meaning of marriage as the center of our sexuality.

THREE

Sex As Sign and Symbol

Our struggle with sex is at least partly that we have forgotten what it means. We have changed its original, biblical meaning into a simple quest for pleasure for everyone. We have said, "What it means is fun, simply giving vent to our deepest physical urges. Everybody has them. Everybody has a right to express sexual feelings and to do it, with whomever they like."

With this "sex for everybody" philosophy has come a tolerance that accepts everything that everybody does as perfectly all right—something about which the bystander is supposed to have no opinion. Everything is relative, they say. Everything is acceptable. Nothing is out of bounds. We are expected to be tolerant of every behavior.

For this reason people sometimes fear that ministers will be "judgmental," so committed to their biblical view of life that they will judge or disagree with other moral or ethical views. Ministers are seen as devoid of the "tolerant" spirit on which American society counts today, the spirit that says, "Anything anybody does is OK." They are suspected of not having the flexibility or the grace to accept people or ideas different from theirs.

I often meet with a strange resistance when I reach the desk of the alcoholic treatment centers in my city and announce that I am a minister and would like to see a parishioner who is a patient there. Often I find that the counselors are reluctant to allow me to see the parishioner. I have learned that it is because I am a minister.

One counselor at a treatment center in a church-related hospital challenged me when I wanted to see a certain patient.

"Well, I am her minister," I suggested. "And I am here because we love her and want her to know that we do, and that Jesus does. I want to encourage her and pray for her."

"How do I know what you're going to do to her?" the counselor replied. "After all, you're into sin and judgment and all that."

"You mean that in this great hospital, founded by the Christian church, with all its protestations about 'the healing team' working together for the patient's good," I said, "that I, as this person's own minister, am not considered part of that team, with a right to come and pray for and encourage someone whose healing is going to come through faith, as well as through the therapies of A.A. and hospital treatment?"

"Well," he said testily, "you're into religion, and we're into spirituality."

I was suspect because I am a minister, someone who was not expected to have the humane compassion that a patient with the disease of alcoholism needed.

Much the same is true in relation to sex. If the prevailing philosophy of the society is that all behavior must be tolerated, then anybody committed to a particular moral view of life is suspect. Since my life is given to tolerating all sorts of people and loving them, no matter who they are or what they've done, I resent the implication both that tolerance is the greatest virtue of our time and that I, by my job and commitment, am incapable of being tolerant.

Gone are the beliefs that good people do bad things, that we can love the sinner without having to love the sin, that life does have consequences, that what we do does make a difference, that how we regard people and deal with them may make all the difference in the world.

Today, however, the aging prophets of the "new morality" have an uneasy vision of the consequences of that free philosophy as they see it working out in the lives of their children. Now they are beginning to say, "Maybe we need standards after all. Maybe there is a right and a wrong, a good and a bad, in finding a way to live with our sexuality."

The important question is what sexuality means. If it means only pleasure now—take what we can get when we can get it—then sex becomes cynical and predatory, abusive and selfish, shallow and mechanistic. But if it means something deep in life, if it has to do with our very soul and commitment and loyalty and our truest love, then it is something to be handled with great care and with immense respect.

In answer to the Pharisees about divorce and about God's intention for men and women at the creation, Jesus maintained that God wanted commitment of a man to a woman and a woman to a man, and that the commitment of their lives to each other was demonstrated and symbolized by the act of becoming "one flesh," of their bodies being physically united, made one. This is a powerful symbol, the symbol of two people's commitment to each other, a commitment the church and the society have both called "marriage." Sexual intercourse is not a sign of lust or love, but a sign of marriage.

What Happens to Signs?

What happens to signs and symbols when they are used for something else for which they were not intended? They lose their power to do the good work they were intended to do.

We live by symbols. The cars we drive, the clothes we wear, the houses we live in, the carpets and furniture and appointments of our offices—all are highly symbolic.

The wedding ring is still a powerful symbol, so powerful that some men I know take their wedding ring off their finger when they go on a business trip out of town. They take their wedding ring seriously enough to believe that that simple piece of metal on their finger has power. For one thing, it can make a woman think twice before accepting a sexual offer from an obviously married man. That ring represents something: a promise made, a love pledged, a life given, an honor intended. It therefore has power to make people feel uncomfortable, to make them feel guilty, to have the effect of cramping their style, of taking away their "freedom," of making them remember the woman and the relationship and the love that that ring symbolizes. That little band of gold is a powerful symbol.

A middle-aged man came into my study one evening to talk about his marriage. Bill was a professional man, with a reasonably important position in a large firm. He was pleasant, calm, cool, and in control, as I find many business people to be. He even seemed a rather placid personality—not someone who was aggressive by nature, or who would enjoy confrontation, but his story was of seething anger, of a grudge held for many of the 20 years of his marriage.

Jane, his wife of all those years, had greatly embarrassed him at a company party in their early years. He had been young and on the make professionally. She had become drunk, gotten sick, and, in his view, had ruined his career—at least in that company. In offering the litany of Jane's various offenses over the years, he described her, among other things, as a "motor mouth." She talked too much.

It was his way of dealing with the original offense that fascinated me. That very night he had quietly removed his wedding ring, placed it in a drawer, and had never worn it again in all those 20 years.

Jane, of course, noticed its absence. "Why won't you wear your wedding ring?" she frequently asked him.

Always he gave an excuse. "It hurts my finger. It's too small. I don't need it to show I love you," were among his various dodges.

That she could have missed his obvious hurt and displeasure, I can hardly believe, but he succeeded in divesting himself for all those years of any visible sign of attachment to Jane. In his own mind, secretly, and without ever openly voicing it, Bill had removed himself from Jane and from any inner sense of obligation to her—20 years earlier.

He had not told her of his displeasure. He had not ranted and raved, nor had he tried in any way to take out this "sin" of his wife, and look at it, and try to be reconciled with her. He simply removed himself from the marriage, in heart and spirit, until that time when their children would be grown and he could finally act on his inner determination to be rid of this person who had so offended him.

In fact, he never gave her a chance. He never allowed her the opportunity for redemption. He determined that she would ultimately pay for her offense.

This was grossly unfair of him—both to her and to himself—but he brought it off by dealing with the symbol. The removal of the ring became the removal of himself from the relationship and its attendant obligations.

Words also stand for something. Like rings, they are symbols. They represent meaning. They have power to make certain things happen.

Remember the story of the shepherd boy who cried "wolf"? It was a great word, with power to call the villagers running to his rescue, if he used it in a moment of danger. For fun he used it when there was no danger. "Wolf!" he cried, "Wolf, wolf!" And the villagers came running, eager and ready to help. The shepherd boy just laughed.

Later, he tried it again. "Wolf, wolf!" he cried, all for fun, just a joke. The villagers came running, and he laughed again.

Then he used the word a third time when there really was a wolf. He called and called, but no one came. "He is only joking," the villagers said to each other. "He intends to laugh at us."

So the shepherd and the sheep were both devoured. The word had lost its power to bring help. The boy had changed the meaning of that tremendously powerful word. He made it what he intended—a joke. That meant it couldn't go back to its original purpose. It couldn't mean what it had first meant. It had been "de-meaned," made less meaningful, given a different and lesser meaning. And it cost the boy his life and the village its flock of sheep.

We can see the same point in the way the King James Version translates the commandment, "Thou shalt not take the name of the Lord thy God in vain." "In vain" means to render powerless, to take away the power of that name to do what it was meant to do. If you curse with the name of Christ, you have used the power in the name negatively. But don't then expect to bless someone with the same name. You have used the name "in vain." Its positive power to bless has been taken away by its negative use as a curse.

Words have power. They are symbols that can do much good, if used positively, but their meaning can also be taken away. They can lose their power to do the good they were intended to do.

Sex As a Sign

What if sexual intercourse is, in the same way, a symbol and a sign—a symbol meant to represent the unity between two people in marriage, a sign that has power to create and underscore and recreate the unity of those two people?

What if sex was given not only for joy, for release, and for therapeutic freeing, for wonderful nonverbal communication of the deepest feelings and intentions between those two, but also as a means to help keep alive that very same intention—to remind them again and again that they are one, that they belong to each other, that they have pledged to stand by each other forever?

Think what it means for a couple in a marriage, when day is done and work is over, to take each other in their arms in the privacy of their bedroom—or anywhere else in their home that they might choose to do it—and hold and fondle and caress each other, telling each other how much the other one means. And finally, to literally enter into each other's bodies and share in that exploding orgasmic sensation of being joined together, bonded in body, each to the other! What an experience! What a powerful, *bonding*, beautiful experience of physically demonstrating what their hearts feel! What an ecstasy to share!

Surely, two people who express love to each other in that way on a frequent basis have found a way to express something of the heart that is almost inexpressible any other way. That act, and the willingness to enter into it with love and joy, says far more than simply, "You're beautiful, and I can't resist your bod!" It even says something more than, "I love you and I want to be with you." It says—by a physical act—"I am you. I am part of you. I enter into you, because I belong to you. We are one. Our physical uniting is a sign of our spiritual uniting. We belong to each other."

It is saying: "My relation with you is not fly-by-night. This is not a one-night stand. I am yours forever. I am part of you. I will be here in the morning. I will be responsible to you. I will support you, stand by you, be with you in your need. If a baby comes as a happy by-product of this act, I will be with you in loving and caring for that child. I am with you—forever!"

The act says something about relationship. The act implies intimacy, depth, permanence, commitment. And the Bible and human society have said, "Commitment *is* marriage."

In its biblical understanding, sexual intercourse is to create and promote the unity, or oneness, of two people in marriage. It is to build up loyalty and symbolize the very ground of their trust for each other.

George and Jean were a couple in their late 30s who fell in love with each other. George had been married once and had a teenage daughter whom he had not seen in many years. Jean had remained single, though she had had one or two affairs, had once been raped by a friend, and had even fallen into a long-term sexual relationship with her psychiatrist.

Jean was confused and hungry for love. George came along and offered himself to her, and in spite of his colorful and questionable background, she took him.

They couldn't resist each other sexually, or at least Jean was too afraid to because she feared she might lose George. So, in spite of some lingering early-life convictions about sex and marriage from her Christian upbringing, she invited George into her home, and they lived together sexually for some months before finally marrying.

Their sexual times in this live-in relationship were "wild, free, and wonderful." But, by their own account, something strange happened once they married. All of a sudden their wonderful sexual life ground to a halt. For a time, it dropped to zero.

At first they couldn't understand it. Then it began to dawn on them. They had done something to that wonderful act. They had made it something different from what they had wanted. They expected it to be the heart of their marriage, but they had made it the heart of their uncommitted affair. They had made it the sign and symbol of something less than marriage, less than commitment.

Once they were married and truly one, all sorts of feelings poured in. But they had nothing else to give, no priceless treasure to offer as the sign and seal of their new relationship. They had trouble making marriage into something different from the affair. Something that they wanted to mean permanence and commitment and unity seemed to have lost its power to do that. By using it in another and lesser way they had changed its meaning.

They found their way back, and they are still married. But they learned that they had violated something they really cared about. Their advice to all their friends who were planning to marry became, "Don't do it before marriage—save it. Save it, so it can mean what you want it to mean."

If sexual intercourse is used before marriage, outside of marriage, its whole purpose is changed. Its meaning is reduced from being a sign of commitment to merely being a sign of love or, much more commonly, a sign only of desire—of the fulfillment of pleasure, even selfish pleasure.

We learn by doing. If we teach ourselves that an act means one thing, we may think that in another context it can mean something else, something higher, something lovelier. But in fact, the meaning has been changed. In our society, sexual intercourse has been shorn of its older, truer meaning. It has been "de-meaned," lessened, cheapened in its meaning. Sex, then, is becoming more and more "used" in film and ad, in magazine and conversation, for ends other than its intended one. The act of intercourse has been so drained of its meaning that it is now something you do with anyone. It is no longer even a revealing, intimate act that shows your inmost heart to another. People reveal only their bodies, not their hearts.

For many today, prayer is much more revealing, and therefore more frightening and forbidding. Prayer is the true "intercourse," the communing of one being with another. But so often sexual intercourse no longer creates communion and communication between two people. It has been made a thing, a mechanistic thing that you do.

Marriage without Symbol

The loss, then, is to marriage. The key relationship is damaged. The dream cherished in one way or other, for some time or other, in all of our lives is devastatingly diminished. The heart of it, the very symbol and sign of it, is taken away. It is still there as an act, but it doesn't mean the same.

More than that, it cannot do for the marriage what it was intended to do. It cannot defend the marriage as it was meant to. It cannot build it up, support it, and deepen it, as it could have done if the act of intercourse had been preserved for its original intention.

I believe our society has failed to understand how much we count on sexual intercourse to be a guard, a hedge, a defense for our marriages. Somehow we've thought we could do anything we wanted with sex and that nothing else would be harmed—as if that intimate act has nothing to do with relationships.

What many couples who come to be married have forgotten, or never quite appreciated, is that marriage is no longer defended by the law, nor by money, nor by corporate life, nor even very well by families. It is too easy to become unmarried today. The law aids and abets the breaking of marriages. Corporate life feels it cannot care about the marriages of its employees. It used to, and it may again, as it realizes how important happy relationships are at home to production at work. Certainly, companies are now recognizing the threat of alcoholism to their employees. They also are beginning to acknowledge new family patterns that demand that they provide on-site nursery care. But they haven't yet felt it important to support and defend and enhance the marriages of their employees.

So it's up to the couples themselves. They need to realize that long-term marriage depends on *trust* and *loyalty*—intangible qualities that cannot be seen, but that are very powerful. Trust and loyalty are built by the habit of being trustworthy and loyal. They grow out of faithfulness, out of commitment. This means we need the words and acts that show commitment. You cannot say "I love you" too many times.

By the same token, you cannot have sex together too many times. It is a binding act, a unifying gesture. It says unity. It speaks oneness, commitment, and intimate identity with the other. But if it's shared around with a variety of people, it simply doesn't mean the same after a while. It loses its power to bind, to unite, to speak oneness.

At the recommendation of Susan's older sister, she and John came to me one night to talk about getting married. Susan came from a family of high faith and commitment. Hers was a hardworking farm family who were deeply involved in their village church. Somehow at age 23 Susan had become involved with John, who was 17. She was infatuated with this boy, fell into a sexual relationship with him, and soon discovered she was pregnant.

The family was aghast at the immaturity of the relationship, and particularly hoped I might discourage the marriage the two young people wanted, and also persuade them to give up the baby for adoption.

John, however, was adamant about marrying Susan and being father to the baby who was coming. Susan, too, felt John was the man for her and that marriage was the only way.

I looked for something in their relationship that might make for permanence in their marriage, that might be a basis for long-term commitment between these two.

John was very quick to say, "Oh, I know I'll stand by Susan whatever comes. I love her more than anybody I've ever had a relationship with, and I'm ready to be a husband and a father."

To try to determine the degree of his commitment to Susan, in contrast to the others with whom he'd had a relationship, and to try to get at what commitment meant to John, I said, "Now, you don't have to answer this, but you've spoken of other 'relationships' you've had and how much more Susan means to you compared to them. Can you tell me how many of them there have been, and, if you don't mind, with how many of these people you have had sex?"

John had to think for several seconds before he said, "Oh, I've had sex with about 40 different girls."

Susan replied, "I've had sex with only about six different men."

Here were two young people who believed they were now in love with each other forever, when one of them, at age 17, had already had sex with 40 women, and the other, the older and more mature one, had been to bed with six men.

I told them I'd love to help them, but that their record of promiscuity and indiscriminate relationships showed that they weren't able, at this point, even to know what a permanent, committed relationship would be, much less to be able to enter into one. I pleaded with Susan to carry the baby to full term, put the baby up for adoption, and not marry John. I suggested they give themselves time to grow up and live apart to see if, after several years, they still felt committed to each other enough to consider marriage.

The act of sex, as they understood it, was so common, so casual, that it hadn't a chance of being a binding force that would hold them together and give strength and permanence to their marriage relationship. They didn't understand what it was or what it was meant to do for them.

Couples who live together before marriage, or at least those who share in sexual intercourse while intending eventually to marry, are often the first to want intercourse to change its meaning and to become that sacred, unifying bond in the marriage that they had really always wanted it to be. They thought that in taking to themselves the pleasure of sex before marriage, they were simply borrowing ahead of time on something that would be good forever. They hadn't bargained on the thing itself changing. As they prepared for their marriage by plans and invitations and dresses and dinners, they didn't realize that they were undercutting their marriage, pulling out the very foundations by teaching themselves the lesser meaning of sexual intercourse. They made it symbolize something far less in their relationship, and in their own minds they took away its association with marriage.

In other words, they taught themselves the "OK-ness" of having intercourse with someone to whom they were not married. They might have sex with quite a few people before they settled down to one person and finally married him or her. But, once married, we have a different expectation of that act, don't we? "Now we belong to each other. And, of course, we wouldn't now have sex with anybody else, would we? We wouldn't share this lovely, intimate thing with someone outside the marriage, would we?"

"Certainly not!" I've heard some couples say. "I'd kill him if he ever went to anybody else. I'd be crushed. Our marriage would be broken forever."

But why? Surely, if two people had sex with each other before marriage, sex without benefit of clergy must be OK. After all, you don't have to be married to someone to have sex with him or her, the argument goes.

"But once we're married, I want my husband to be faithful just to me!" But that isn't what you prepared for, is it? In fact, you prepared the way for a life of unfaithfulness, of what the Bible calls adultery—an adulterated relationship—one that can hardly expect purity of act and purpose.

The couples coming to me for premarriage counseling believe they will never be unfaithful. What they have not prepared for is the day of anger and hurt, when they want to get back at the other, when they feel done in by, or ignored by the other. That is the danger time. Why should old patterns and old philosophies not reappear then? Anything you did once, you can do again. If you accepted adultery or fornication before marriage, you can always come around to it again.

So every marriage, entered into by partners who have used sex as something less than an act of unity in marriage, is threatened even before it has begun. And the marriage partners are tragically unaware of what they've done. They cannot understand how trust and loyalty could break down later in their years together. They can scarcely believe their partner could commit adultery. Yet, in fact, they had asked for it, set themselves up for it, programmed it.

This does not mean adultery has to be the end of the marriage. If there is faith and a shared love for God, a practice of prayer, and an ability to turn to the one who is the source of love and from whom all goodness comes— their marriage could be healed. They could forgive, and go on. But what a big *if!* What a high risk!

The lack of faith shared, and the lack of a high view of sexual intercourse as sacred symbol, sacrament, or a holy thing are the two factors that have condemned many modern marriages to disintegration and disaster. That, in fact, is what we are seeing now. Three out of every five marriages are ending in divorce. In many of those marriages adultery in one form or another is present, and often because the deep, symbolic meaning of sexual intercourse has not been understood.

FOUR

A Reason for Waiting

For a couple soon to be married, or for a young person in love and hoping one day for marriage, or for any of the rest of us, married or unmarried, the question is, Does the meaning of sexual intercourse call me to deal with it differently than I would if it had no particular meaning? If it really is a sign of commitment in marriage and not something appropriate for other relationships, does that make me want to treat it in a different way?

It's a very pragmatic question. What do you really want in your life? What do you most value? What do you want to have count for you in life?

All kinds of people, both young and far from young, come to see me about getting married, and for many, it's the first time. But for an increasing number, it's the second time or the third time. The fact that I am marrying people the third time around doesn't mean that I or the church have no principles, or that we don't care, or that we are not defending true, one-time, forever marriage. We do it because we believe Jesus and the gospel bids for the future, that Christian faith is always seeking to redeem, to buy back, to offer the second chance, the opportunity to start over.

"Lord, how many times shall I forgive my brother when he sins against me?" Peter asked Jesus. "Up to seven times?"

Jesus' simple answer was, "Not seven times, but seventy-seven times" (Matt. 18:21-22). In other words, as many times as that person needs to be forgiven.

Jesus is not indiscriminating, but he wants to hold out hope, to keep people living, and not giving up or despairing. Nor does the church and its faith mean to encourage turning in the old wife or husband for a new model, just because the old one has become uninteresting or even a pain in the neck. Divorce is not a simple answer for people today any more than it was in Jesus' day. (At that time it was permitted, and on the most cruelly chauvinistic basis imaginable. A mere piece of paper handed by a husband to his wife, stating his desire to be done with her, was all that Jewish law required for a divorce at the beginning of the first century.)

My experience is that most people made a far better choice of a partner for life when they were in their early 20s than they give themselves credit for. That person is often more akin to the real values of our inner heart than are those more exotic folks we tend to tie up with later in life. There is more innocence and more sheer joy in "the bride of one's youth" than in the mid-life people who come along and often appeal to the darker side of one's nature. The untouched, struggling soul within does need expression, but it doesn't need a new partner as much as it thinks it does.

The tragedy is in what has happened to that early love. What awful taking for granted, sameness of life, or dulling of spirit has been allowed to happen to curse that once-bright, beautifully romantic, wonderfully hopeful partnership?

How does such anger, such stony cold silence, even such vengeful spirit, come to people once so much in love? Is it because they are bad people, selfish and mean, always pouty and angry? Almost never so.

Rather, something happens between two perfectly well-intentioned and usually deeply in love people that seems baffling to the outside observer. Everything comes crashing down in their marriages when we least expect it. Everything seemed to be "going for them," as we say. They were just starting off in life, often had quite good jobs, were reasonably healthy, beautiful, frequently well-educated, and—very much in love. What could possibly go wrong? How could anything come between them?

These people are, if anything, typical products of our self-centered, highly-trained, great-expectation society. They are programmed for the fast track. They are going to be successful, and they know it. Their trap is that they believe their success too much. They trust too much in it. They think they are so worldly wise that they have it made. They trust too much their own goodness, their own ability and strength. They believe, as our society has taught them, that "communication is the answer," that acquiring the right skills in relationships and communication—"dealing with your anger," "letting it all hang out," and "being in touch with your feelings"—that these techniques and ways of talking will solve it all for them.

While those may be good techniques, these people often miss something far deeper. They frequently are trapped in trusting themselves, in trusting their own goodness, in trusting their love for each other. "We will succeed because we are so good together, because of our great love, because we communicate so well" is their naive answer to why they are going to "make it" in the long haul of marriage.

The Importance of Shared Faith

Sandy was nervous when she came around one Saturday morning, bringing George along for their first counseling appointment prior to their wedding (tentatively scheduled for three months later). She desperately hoped that I would like and approve of George. She also hoped that he would not be put off by my faith stance and would like me in the same way she did.

She and I had been friends for a long time. A plain but elegant young woman, Sandy came from a reserved, professional family and was already making a good career for herself. She was deeply sincere and had been in love before.

In fact, she had come once before with another man for a similar premarriage counseling session. She and he had both shared an authentic Christian faith, and his gentle spirit had had great appeal to her. But as time had gone on, she had come to see that this man she loved so much, who had been married and divorced but who seemed so devoted to her, would never talk about her to his friends. He seemed unwilling to acknowledge that he was in love with someone or that he had, in fact, verbally committed himself to marrying her. He never seemed quite ready to finally set the date. Finally she discovered that for all his sensitivities and wistful, wonderful spirit, he was psychologically incapable of taking on a commitment in marriage. Believing this man was going to be her husband, she had put aside her own deeply held convictions about sexual abstinence before marriage and had consented to sleeping with him a number of times.

When the marriage plans hadn't worked out, she had felt used and abused. Now, here she was, finally ready to try again with another man.

The trouble with this young man, however, was that while her new choice for a partner was wonderful in every respect—highly educated, already succeeding in business, and showing a high degree of family loyalty—he was not a convinced Christian. He was inclined to be skeptical about the faith.

Sandy knew I believed that a shared faith was essential to the success of any marriage. Clearly, she wanted me to accept him and to open him to the Christian persuasion.

George certainly was a fine young man. He had all the talents she said he had. He seemed to love her, but he would form a marriage without the faith dimension. In his view, they had such a good relationship and were so well suited to each other that he didn't see any need to have a shared faith for their marriage to be successful. "I certainly support Sandy in her faith, and in her wanting to go to church, and all that," he said. "But I'm not ready yet to commit myself to faith. Sandy and I will have a good marriage because we love each other, because we are well-educated, reasonable people, and because we understand each other, and can talk out easily any differences we may have."

It sounded so plausible. And Sandy wanted so much to believe that it was really OK and was really all she had hoped for. But they didn't come back. A few weeks later we learned that the wedding had been cancelled.

Sandy has never told me why. I think she knew that it takes something more than good communication, education, and job stability. Sharing the faith was important to her, and after being stung once in a relationship, she wasn't ready to chance a marriage with someone who trusted only in his own goodness and ability and success.

The truth is that nobody makes it in marriage on his or her own. None of us do it on our own strength and skill and know-how and great communication ability. In fact, I consider it a miracle anybody stays married today, because ours has become an essentially predatory society.

The society no longer feels it has anything invested in the success of the basic institution of marriage and the family. Business has accepted the notion that "whatever you do outside the office is your own business. We're not interested in your moral life, your private ethics, the forms or practices of your personal sexuality, the affairs you have, the way you treat your children, or how you deal with your neighbors. Our interest is solely in how you perform for our company." That cynical, dichotomizing view of human life now dominates American business and professional life. It's as if your private morality and ethics has no bearing on your public or professional ethic, as if you could be an essentially different person for the company than you are for your wife or husband, as if your infidelities at home would never make for unfaithfulness in your professional or business responsibilities.

This is a dangerous and unrealistic view of human life and nature. It also means that the business and professional world has no interest in defending or supporting its employees' marriages. Divorce is seen as purely private. You don't lose your job for it anymore. You can even be a Protestant minister and not necessarily lose your job should you have a failed marriage, an ensuing divorce, or even an affair along the way. Affairs are largely countenanced in the world of American business and professions today. Men and women see nothing wrong with any sort of social relationship with an attractive person at work— even with the development of increasing intimacies. Being married and wearing a wedding ring no longer automatically takes one out of circulation.

There are threats to all our marriages that were not there in the same way 30 years ago. Even one's own family— the folks back home—are far less likely to go to bat for our marriages than they once were. They are now far more likely to wistfully shrug their shoulders and say something like, "The kids are having trouble with their marriage. But what can we do? We certainly don't want to interfere."

Tolerance has taught us not only our right to "do our own thing" no matter who is hurt, but has taught us, too, that other people's problems and struggles are no affair of ours. "They have to work it out for themselves" is a modern rationalization, designed to relieve us of any sense of responsibility for others or for the world. We wanted to become a guiltless society, and we've done it—in spite of all our talk about the importance of relationships.

All of which means that people marrying today have many more threats to their marriage, more factors working against the possibility of their succeeding, than was true a few decades ago. The newly married couple will be mobile, probably both working, both having cars, and often traveling at great distances from each other, perhaps even living apart from each other for extended times because of business and vacation conflicts. And in a world deeply influenced by the values of television talk-show hosts and publishers of magazines, the reasons for being faithful to a marriage partner, either in the heart and mind or physically in sexual ways, are much less persuasive than they were even 20 years ago.

The heart plays havoc with the whole of life. Our assumptions about life and relationships and commitment to each other and shared values mean everything. We are utterly dependent for the success of our marriages not on our good looks, our abilities and skills, our intelligence, our communication skills, or even our love for each other, but on our values, our ideals, and on what we believe is important in life. These are what we live by. These will determine what we will do to each other, how we will regard and care for each other, and how faithful we will be to each other.

Loyalty and trust are the dimensions of value and of the kind of relationships that every one of us needs for our marriages, whether we are young and just being married or older and married many years. Trust and loyalty come from sources beyond us. Faithfulness, the willingness to stand by another even when he or she is fat and no longer beautiful, or is sick, or sad, or weary, or worried, or not as much fun as before, or unemployed, or alcoholic, or just plain no longer interesting, comes from a source beyond ourselves.

Love, after all, runs out. People do get tired of each other. Married people hurt each other, are cruel to each other—intentionally or not. Ordinary mortals—especially those of us living longer than earlier generations—become weary of well-doing toward each other. We may even just plain tire of each other.

Tired marriages are all around me. Boring ones are there, too, and so are silent, angry marriages.

When Alice came to town a decade ago, her husband had a responsible executive position. Don was a somewhat placid man, aggressive neither at home nor at work.

Although she was a financially well-off suburban woman "who had everything," Alice felt that she had an unexciting husband. She was frightened at being home in her big house when Don was on business trips, and she found quite a few reasons to feel sorry for herself. She tried to get back at Don for being a dull fellow by cutting him out sexually. And, horror of horrors, Don didn't even seem to notice.

The result was a dull, unspoken stand-off, with Don paying the bills, keeping Alice in nice clothes and high style, but with little affection or even friendship between them. "Don and I haven't had sex together in 15 years!" Alice confessed one day.

Nor is she the only person to have reported the same tired, tedious stand-off in a marriage.

So what is to hold two people together in a marriage? How are they to stick it out? What will keep them hanging on when things get tough? The law surely won't keep them together. Extended families won't. The corporation won't. Original good intentions won't. Even the love of their courtship and early marriage won't. Witness the number who are getting unmarried. There seems little to stem the tide.

If we are to depend only on ourselves, our own human strength, wisdom, love, and good sense, we are likely to fail and fall apart, precisely because we are human, because in being human we are tempted to think of ourselves first, and watch out for ourselves alone. Most of us are cut off from our sources, which means most of all, cut off from God. We are out of touch with the very one who promised to give us life, life in all its fullness, the one who said we could "ask anything" and we would receive it, the one who said, "I am the light of the world." If we want light and life, God is the source. God is the one to go to. God is the dimension that can bring sanity into our marriages. If we lose our love for each other, we can go to God for more and better, because God is love.

A mutual trust in someone outside and beyond our marriage, who is the source of life and love, is critical if we want to have our old and tired and broken and even lost love restored, or better yet, replaced by a new, fresh, deeper, wiser love.

This is a plea for a humble spirit of openness to God, of willingness to ask help and to look daily for help from one whom all of us need in our marriages. We will never make it on our own.

The question is, How much do people really want a marriage at all? How great a value is that personal, deep, enduring relationship of commitment to and with another person?

If it's important enough, if its value is high enough, if a happy, lifetime marriage is perceived as a sufficiently worthy, worthwhile, and wonderful goal, then maybe people will be willing to get very serious about doing what is necessary to attain it and maintain it.

Every couple I have ever married has always wanted to be married for life. Prior to their marriage not one of them ever said that they really wanted only to be married for a few years—just "as long as we both shall love," or as long as the other one was still beautiful or fun or interesting. They all say they want to be married forever. They all say they want to grow old together. They all say they want to be faithful to the end. They all say they love each other dearly, and want it to work—especially those who have been married before, when it didn't work.

If faith in God might help them achieve that, it would seem to me worth a try. It might be worth being willing to pray together, frightening as that prospect might be. If they could learn more about this God of love in the Bible, it might be worth trying to read that book together.

The issue, of course, is how much difference does it make, and what are the real values, the things we really put store by, for which we really might make sacrifice? Is marriage—and as part of that, the family—that kind of ultimate value for us?

Pilgrims and Seekers

The fact that so many people are still getting married, in spite of the ominous statistics against its success, is powerful evidence that marriage is one thing many people care deeply about. They do want the permanent, intimate, upholding, and partnerly relationship that marriage can be.

They might even be willing to make some significant sacrifices in order to assure, or at least hold out some hope for, its success.

Many a couple with no religious background or conviction has suddenly made the connection, has seen what had never seemed important to them before—that a relationship as precious as marriage does depend on values, and that faith may really be the source of those values. They have agreed to become pilgrims, seekers in the matter of faith, to explore what it might mean for them.

David and Sondra had met as college students and were both intellectual and well-educated.

David dutifully came to go through the process of marriage counseling at Sondra's home church. He wasn't enthusiastic about the process, and he confessed to having been away from church for some years. He certainly did not want to settle down in Sondra's town, or become part of the church where she had grown up and where her family was still very active.

Sondra held to her faith. David could at least see that it was an important part of her life. Perhaps for that reason alone, he decided to learn what he could about this thing called religion. He grudgingly began coming to worship with Sondra. Gradually his coming wasn't grudging. Soon he began to be engaged intellectually by the assumptions of faith. Before long, it had taken hold of his heart and began to help him in his life.

As time went on, friendships, activities, and events of all kinds were centering in the church for them. That fact, as well as the philosophical and theological assumptions of faith, and the more and more regular practice of it, particularly through prayer in their home, began to draw David and Sondra together in a new set of assumptions about life. It became part of their home and family. The convictions of faith were what they passed on to their children. Both of these young parents became leaders in the church. Their marriage continues to deepen and grow.

Couples can pray. They can be willing to seek God. They can give the Bible and the church a chance in their lives.

Gain through Sacrifice

But the tougher question for many unmarried couples has been, would they give up the sexual relationship of intercourse which so many of them had already made part of their lives, as if they were already married?

Would they make this sacrifice if they thought that giving up this treasured, fulfilling act of love would bring long-term gain—the health and permanence of the marriage into which they were about to enter? That is the central question for all of us when we raise the question of standards and principles in the exercise and fulfillment of our sexuality.

The issue isn't whether sex is good and beautiful and full of wonder and something God wants for everyone. The question is whether sexual intercourse is indeed the unique act and sign of marriage, and therefore ought to be reserved for marriage so it can do its work of symbolizing and defending and protecting that marriage.

Nobody wants to destroy the power of the thing that has been given to help them. Nobody wants to cut himself or herself off from the very door to life which one is preparing so eagerly to enter.

If sexual intercourse is the sign and seal of marriage and not of love or desire, and if its unique power to heal and restore and deepen a marriage, and to protect it from all those threats that will surely come from the outside as well as the inside in every couple's life, then it may well be eminently worth giving up present pleasure in order to receive that long-term gain.

What I suggest to young couples is that they back off from their live-in relationship or their occasional sexual intercourse, and abstain from it until the day of their marriage, thus giving that act a chance to recover for them its intended meaning, to be seen by them in a new light, to gain for them a new power, a new honor, a new integrity.

Many things, after all, gain value by the amount of sacrifice made to achieve them. The present interest in running, for instance, and the entering of thousands in marathon races, is a good example of this. Runners sacrifice all sorts of things—sometimes even sex—for the sake of getting in shape to run an important race. We sacrifice to earn a graduate degree, to learn to play an instrument, to write a book, to do anything well. We wouldn't dream of taking to ourselves the badge of honor, the sign or symbol of that great and hard-won achievement before we had actually fulfilled the goal. Only those who win in the Super Bowl have the right to wear the ring as sign and symbol of that victory. Only those who earn the degree wear the academic hood.

We are serious about these signs and seals. Why are we not serious about the sign and seal of marriage, sexual intercourse? Perhaps because we have forgotten that it is the sign and symbol of marriage. We let American advertising, and the talk-show hosts, and the *Playboy* philosophy, and situation ethics, and the new morality tell us that sexual intercourse is everybody's right and everybody's privilege. They cut away its meaning and told us essentially that that beautiful act meant nothing, or at least meant something different and something less. Because it has come to mean less, it came to have no power in our marriages to protect us, and hedge us round, and make us safe in our life of love with our partner.

If we want it back, and see now that it has deep meaning, that it is a significant sign and symbol that we want for our marriages—then we may be ready to do almost anything to restore that deep marriage-meaning to sexual intercourse, and so to give it for us a new meaning, one that perhaps we always thought it should have.

This is the case for not having sexual intercourse before marriage, the case for virginity, the case for abstinence and sacrifice. It is all because of something we'd like this beautiful act to mean for us, a meaning that because of the act's misuse has been lost.

Many a couple has told me, "You know, we did what you said. We had never understood it before, but it made sense. It was what we wanted, because our marriage is everything to us. So we moved out for the last few months. And you know, we feel something has been added back into our relationship and certainly to our marriage. It was hard, but it felt good to be sacrificing something for each other. It added a new integrity and strength to our relationship. Our honeymoon became a real honeymoon."

A cherished and preserved and honored sense of sexuality and a deepened and serious faith in a living and loving God are the two twin foundations for recovering permanence and power in marriage today.

The other day, while I was at breakfast with a staff member at a restaurant, an energetic, middle-aged businessman named Jim stopped at our table and squatted down beside us to make a surprising affirmation. He nodded toward his wife, Cynthia, and their two-year-old daughter. "It's her second birthday. We're celebrating this morning with breakfast out, all together."

Given Jim's background, it was an amazing domestic scene. When I first knew him two and a half years ago, Jim was a recovering alcoholic. His life was in turmoil. Although he was successful in his business, his life was in a shambles. He had been divorced for several years, but

had been living with a young woman whom he had expected eventually to marry and who had reason enough
to believe that was his intention.

On the other hand, there was Cynthia, a work colleague
who had become not only a friend and soul mate, but also
his occasional partner in bed. They had talked about many
things, and found they had much in common, including
a yearning for faith, something he had not shared with
the young woman with whom he lived.

To complicate it all, Cynthia now was pregnant. He felt
he loved her and was sure he would love that little child.
But the pregnancy would cost Cynthia her job, and if their
relation with each other should become known, it might
cost him his job as well. And he also cared for the young
woman with whom he was living, the one who thought
sooner or later she would be Jim's wife.

What was he to do? Marry one and dream forever about
the other? Or abandon one, marry the other, but feel guilty
forever about the jilted one? How could he ever have
gotten himself into such a plight?

We labored long over this one. Rather than seek an
immediate solution, we looked first at faith. "Start there,"
I said to Jim. "Give your heart to God, and let him begin
to sort this out." And so it began.

Months later, Jim came to see me with Cynthia in tow.
He was going with his friend, the one he loved, the one
who was carrying his child. He had dealt as honestly as
he could with his other live-in friend. He had made a start.

Why not now move in with Cynthia? That had been
his style before. It was then that I made the plea of this
chapter to Jim and Cynthia. "What do you want your
marriage to count for, long-term? What do you care about
and really want? As you seek God, what do you need in
order to be right with him? And what about being right
with each other? Maybe you'd feel better and secure a

new life for the marriage you want by going at this one in a new way—through sacrifice, through abstinence, through backing off from your sexual relationship, and giving intercourse a chance to recover its original, biblical meaning, as the sign of something sacred, something that can give integrity and power to your marriage?"

"Arthur," said Jim, squatting there, "don't ever back off from that little speech you gave Cynthia and me two years ago. It was just what we needed, even though it was hard to hear at the time. We have given it over and over again to any number of couples who've talked with us about marriage. It's the only way. It has made all the sense in the world to us, and is, we believe, the hope of our marriage. Don't ever give up on it!"

So a philosophy of abstinence from sexual intercourse before marriage makes it possible for that act to become the great sign of marriage and its commitment again. If mature marriage, the chance to love another human being and live in daily love and joy and service with that person for the rest of your life, is anything our society really wants, then a standard of morality far beyond "not doing it until you're 17" is needed.

This chapter suggests what a *new*, new morality—understood in a far deeper way than either the old, "traditional" morality or the so-called new morality of recent decades—can do to offer a standard, a morality that can make sense for teenagers and for all of us, as we struggle with sex and try to understand what it means and how it can heal our hearts, exhilarate our spirits, and refresh our bodies.

Marriage is the key, as well as how you prepare for it and honor it and give it a chance to be the great knitting relationship of our society.

FIVE

For Those Who Wait

To wait for sexual intercourse until that day of fulfillment in marriage is one thing. To wait with no expectation, or at least no assurance, of a fulfilled relationship of sexual intimacy may be quite another.

For many people today, there is little expectation of marriage. There are many more single households in America than ever before. While many of these are the once-married and now divorced, an increasing number are people never married—the just plain single, who are living out their lives alone.

Teenagers have the world before them, and life seems to promise the eventuality of someone to love and live with. Their lives can be lived with an anticipation and hope of partnership.

Older people, those retired from working lives, now in their 70s or 80s, have reduced opportunity for the prospect of marriage for the first time, if they are not already married. If they are widowed after a long and happy marriage, they have memories they do not want to spoil and a life-time of love that can be lived in reflection. These become reasons for not wanting to marry again.

There are those, too, of all ages, who for reasons of faith and commitment to a life of Christian service in a religious order or simply in a life of faithfulness lived out in the secular world of work, choose not to take on a partner in life, and who, therefore, choose not to seek the pleasure and joy of a sexual relationship with another person.

On top of these realities in American society in the final decades of the 20th century is the strong current of feminism, which, in its more radical forms, has developed a deep suspicion toward men as oppressors and users and manipulators of women, with consequent antipathy on the part of some women toward a sexual relationship with any man—much less with a man taken on permanently in a marriage relationship.

Even for less radical feminists, there is a heightened awareness of the highly sexual overtones of American culture, seen particularly in its advertising, but also in its television soap operas and police shows, where women and their sexuality are exploited and often associated with violence.

Public outcry against rape has caused men as well as women to look deep into the psyche of our time to wonder about those sources of violence within us—particularly of men toward women—and so to feel revulsion at these dimensions of our sexuality. Such revulsion can move both women and men away from openness toward a sexual relationship with a person of the opposite sex—even in a committed relationship of marriage.

Fear and uncertainty about the opposite sex is one of the sources of the urge toward the "gay" life of homosexuality as another possibility for some people. While there are some gay couples—male couples and female couples—the gay life is generally another way of living singly.

For any one of a number of different reasons, many Americans are living singly, either not wanting or not able to enter into a regular, loving, and happy married life of frequent sexual fulfillment through sexual intercourse.

The Need for Sexual Fulfillment

In spite of this increasing singleness, it has come to be widely accepted in America that every person nevertheless has the right to sexual fulfillment.

That is part of the struggle parents now have with teen-age sex. In granting unmarried teenagers the right to full sexual expression, we have come to realize there are huge implications that go beyond the mere act of sexual intercourse: pregnancy, motherhood, fatherhood, family, financial competence, maturity, adoption, abortion, and all the psychic strain and pain associated with each of those realities. To be 18, or 15, or 13 and faced with these issues is nothing short of appalling. So we find ourselves talking again about standards, about principles—even about morality.

Yet the problems of unlimited sexual activity for the young—and for some of the old—are there because of the deep urge within us all to copulate. Something in every one of us wants to reach out and with our bodies to embrace our own human kind—to hold them with arms and legs, with fingers and toes, to be pressed against them, to feel their warmth and oneness with us. Since the creation, there has been a sense of men and women coming from the same flesh, seeking ever to be reunited with each other. "Bone of my bones," cried Adam when presented by God with Eve, formed from his own rib, "and flesh of my flesh"

(Gen. 2:23). Ever since, the human race has wanted to be joined, connected, united.

It is a passion within us that most of us do not understand. St. Paul identified it with fire. "Better to marry than to burn," he said, not meaning to burn in hell, but to burn with passion, with a feeling that can so easily rage out of control (1 Cor. 7:9).

Is it only men who have trouble controlling this passion? Men and women clearly are different in their cycles of emotion and passion. My observation of men and women generally is that women are cyclical—sometimes close and intimate, sometimes regal and reserved, sometimes wild and free. Men, on the other hand, tend for the most part to be constant, which is not to say faithful. But their nature tends towards sameness, the same personality, the same degree of interest, the same excitability or lack of it, the same temperament, the same intensity or lack of it.

These natural human differences show themselves sexually in a tendency for men to be about as ready for sexual stimulation and interest at one time as at another, while women appear to have some far more intense times and other far less intense times. Those differences make for problems in "getting together," even for two people in a marriage—indeed, especially for two people living in a constant, daily relationship of intimacy with each other in the committed context of marriage.

Despite differences in time and intensity, the urge is there for us all. Sexuality and sexual awareness is a universal human language. Everybody knows it, everybody feels it. Taboos may be different in different cultures, but men and women throughout the world think about each other, are intensely interested in each other, and in varying degrees dwell on the features of each others' sexuality, and long to come close to each other in a deep way.

Those Who Wait

Christina wants very much to be married. She is approaching 30 and feels that time is running out. A number of friends her age have already been married and divorced. In some cases they are now single parents of one or two children.

In no way does Christina want their experience. She would rather be single forever than go through the hell those friends have experienced.

On the other hand, she'd love a chance to try, to have a go at living with a man in marriage, at loving him and trying to get along, and seeing if they can be happy together. She'd love to be able to have sex often and freely with someone she respects and loves and to whom she could feel a lifetime commitment. She'd love to be a mother and feels she could be good at it.

Christina isn't single because she's plain, or unattractive, or overweight, or any of those physical drawbacks that are obstacles for some people. Christina is physically attractive, outgoing, full of smiles, fun-loving.

In college and graduate school several men have been drawn to her. In two or three instances, she was drawn to them—for a while. But none of those relationships worked out. In each case she came to realize these men just were not right for her.

She still has hopes. Everyone says, "Your time will come. There is someone, somewhere, out there for you." But what about in the meantime? Christina is a healthy, whole, young woman. She has sexual urges like the rest of us.

In her case, she is not tempted to have sex with someone just for the sake of sex. Yet the urge, the desire, is there. What do we say about that? What does the Bible say and the church believe? What should Christina do?

In every culture taboos, restrictions, standards, and a morality have grown up around sexuality, around the sense that people have some rights simply as human beings. They aren't owned by each other. Certain relationships need to be defined in order to be responsible, to care for the children given birth out of sexual relations, to order the society for work and cooperation through families. So in the many cultures of the world there are many and sometimes strange ways of ordering the relationships that grow from sexual passion.

That modern America proclaims the right of every one of every age and stage to have a sexual life flies in the face of even our society's acknowledgment of a whole network of responsibilities. Yet there is a sense that sexuality is so basic, so precious, so important to all of our personalities that the distortions, misunderstandings, and dark fears foisted on the present middle-aged generation—the postwar young marrieds of the 1950s—largely by the fears and apprehensions and silences of our parents must not be passed along to our children. We've wanted these children to be whole sexual people, with a sense of joy about sex, free from dark inhibitions and fears.

The apparent trouble with this generation, and the younger generation of parents married in the 1960s and 70s, is that we saw no middle ground, no place between complete freedom with no restrictions and complete repression and abstention for no reason other than that "sex is bad," or parents say, "Don't do it," or God or the minister or society says, "Don't do it." The desperate need today is to discover and articulate a middle ground—some position that acknowledges the deep urge for sexual fulfillment within us all, but that acknowledges that relationships demand responsibility and therefore commitment.

All the stung singles who have been married and painfully divorced—often an experience of terrible rejection by a partner—are afraid, or at least hesitant, to enter a marriage relationship where the same thing might happen again.

Mike and Marcia were one of many couples who never quite escaped those ghosts of their past marriages. Mike was strongly built, a rough-and-ready fellow with a tender heart. He had been married before, and had two young teenage children. His first wife was an alcoholic, and the scars of many wounds were deep. The children were apparently pawns for pain between them on a continuing basis. Tears came to Mike's eyes several times as we talked about that marriage and its pain and about the children.

Marcia had also been married, but had no children of her own. She hoped to adopt a minority child whom she had come to love through Big Sisters. It wasn't quite clear how ready Mike was for that.

Marcia and Mike had been living together for some months, with his children in and out of their relationship on a weekend or short-visit basis. Even with their knowing each other that well, Mike and Marcia were not quite sure how it was going to be after they were married. They knew that somehow it would be different and difficult with the children, different with each other.

They confessed their fears to one another. Marcia, a wonderful, hardy woman, who looked as if she could handle anything, always insisted that they "had it made." "It will all work out," she said, over and over again. Yet she never quite knew.

After a couple of early delays, they determined to proceed in faith. It was a risk they felt they had to take, despite the pain of the past and all the negative possibilities of the future.

They did it. The wedding was beautiful. Marcia has been back to talk about her longing for children of her own and the difficulties, legal and otherwise, of adoption. They never backed off from marriage, but they entered it, for the second time, with fears many generations never had. Despite hesitations and delays, people like these never cease to be sexual people.

Teenagers are sexual people, just discovering their sexuality.

Widows and widowers may have enjoyed a wonderful and fulfilling life of sexual intimacy that now is cut off forever. They, too, are still sexual creatures.

The fearful divorced and the singles for whom the right person has not yet come along are nevertheless sexual people, perhaps hoping to be able to give themselves lovingly to another.

The religious celibate and the feminist celibate have strong reasons for abstaining from sexual intercourse with another, yet they, too, are sexual beings.

There are also those who, because of injury or illness, are unable to have sexual intercourse with a marriage partner, yet their sexuality remains.

All these have sexual longings, the desire to be loved, to be held, to know the joy and fulfillment of sexual release within their own bodies and their own spirits.

A Compassionate Alternative

Have they no right to that release, that fulfillment? Are they to have no sexual experience at all, no sense of their own sexuality, their bodily and spiritual fulfillment? Is that, too, part of our moral standard?

For 200 years it has been. Misusing the biblical condemnation of Onan, who "spilled his seed on the ground" rather than complete the act of sexual intercourse (Gen.

38:9), the early 18th century began to build a fear about sexual fondling of one's own genitals, especially by males, prophesying dark disease and malady to befall those who thus indulge themselves. But in his recent book, *Whatever Became of Sin?* Dr. Karl Menninger, renowned psychiatrist and committed Christian and churchman, takes to task the dark fear about that self-exploration and "pleasuring," defends its place in our sexual experience, and pleads for its removal from the code of "don'ts" in the sexual life of our time. In a book that seeks to reinstate a healthy notion of sin and guilt so we can deal psychologically and spiritually with the evil in which we really have participated, Menninger is careful to remove masturbation from the realm of those human acts that should be viewed as sin.

In a society whose penchant in everything seems to be "all or nothing at all," "first in everything or I won't try at all," the "whole shot," "going all the way," "grabbing the gusto because you only go around once," there is a growing need for balance, for temperance, for stages, for development, for appropriate expressions at appropriate levels.

In the light of the social consequences, we should not allow or even encourage teenagers to engage in full sexual intercourse, with all that that means for relationship, for their own human spirits and psyches, and obviously for pregnancy and parenting. They simply are unable in almost any way to fulfill the responsibilities that are the consequences of that act. But to forbid their private sexual exploration of their own bodies is to needlessly, and perhaps cruelly, create at the very beginning of their sexual awakening a sense of darkness, of fear, and sin and even lostness before God.

Many parents have more fear and less freedom to talk about masturbation with their young teenage children than they have about the far more serious and life-changing results of sexual intercourse. Many parents have at least expressed concern about sexual intercourse and pregnancy, and in some cases even offered birth control means to their sons and daughters, but most have been helpless about the issue of "self-pleasuring."

The concerns—religious and moral—of those who teach and preach against it are not without grounds. They fear that boys and girls—or men and women—may become stuck at some lower level of sexual expression that may make them less able to enter fully into a whole human relationship of intercourse in a marriage. Such a concern should be part of our understanding of pleasuring oneself. After all, St. Paul himself said that a husband and wife owe each other their bodies and should be ready freely to give themselves to each other frequently and fully, interrupted only when they have made a mutual decision to go apart for a time for prayer.

All of us want to be free for that whole, full giving of ourselves sexually in marriage to one we love. But even in the most loving and giving marriages there are times of unavoidable separation—a week or two on business trips, absence from each other to fulfill family obligations, much longer and extended trips away for a company or organization, or even temporarily living apart because of the necessities of jobs. Couples in the military have long experienced the pain of extended separation from each other.

In our all-or-nothing world of full sex on demand, it is a terrible temptation to think one's sexuality demands gratification at the highest level and the fullest possible way, whether one is with one's partner or not. This has led to widespread justification either of the affair, or of more fleeting, casual, or even prostituted sexual relationships with other people.

They may talk of "open marriage" and desire to be very liberated and modern about it all, but there is nothing blasé about the relation of two married partners when one of them discovers that the other has been unfaithful sexually to their pledged covenant of commitment to "keep only unto the other." The hurt is deep, often permanent, and frequently destructive of the marriage.

How much better off they would be to acknowledge each other's sexual longing, understand the temporary separation as unavoidable in this fast-moving and pressured society, and reaffirm their devotion and promise to each other, symbolized in the beautiful sign of their shared sexual intercourse with each other, and then grant to each other the right to seek sexual fulfillment by that private, personal, albeit lonely, means that self-pleasuring affords.

Rather than a dark secret withheld from each other, a secret passion fulfilled in those times when separate or when deference to the other's need, or sickness, or weariness, or a temporary lack of interest precludes shared sexual intercourse, how much better an honest, open, joyful permission and even encouragement to the other to release sexual urges in this way that involves neither disloyalty nor adultery with another?

In this day of such pressures and such constant tension in the lives of all of us, it would be an act of compassion and understanding for two people devoted to each other in marriage to grant this kind of freedom to each other, thus obviating the physical need for adultery, which can so easily come when the all-or-nothing principle prevails, when it is sexual intercourse or nothing at all.

The acceptance of the many other pleasures of sex for married people, the fondling and stroking and oral forms of stimulation, are symbolic of a much wider range of sexual experience available to us today. Self-pleasuring can be an honest part of that, even though it is not the most complete and fulfilling form of sexual expression.

If it can help the devoted married couple, can it not also help the single adult who chooses not to be married or has not yet found someone to marry? Or the adult who is divorced and not yet ready to enter into all the commitments and psychic ramifications of another marriage? Or the widow or widower, who wishes to cherish till the end of life the memory of a wonderful and fulfilling marriage, but who still has sexual longings and urges? Or even the celibate, who is committed by faith not to marry, and might be helped to maintain that promise of a life without marriage and without sexual intercourse by the possibility of this occasional private release? And, finally, the awakening teenager, whose urges are sometimes overwhelming, but who wants to keep himself or herself virgin for that one who someday can be approached in love as marriage partner, with their intercourse, so long waited for, standing as sign and seal of their deep and lifelong covenant of commitment to each other?

A Search for Guidelines

Because we fear to think about this for our children or for ourselves, we have failed to offer any guidance for appropriate ways the pleasuring of oneself can be carried on, particularly without offense to others.

A young mother once described her own dealing with her son in this matter. She conveyed not the slightest note of apprehension about it and helped her little boy to think of his desire to fondle his genitals as a perfectly normal thing. It had happened in the home in full view of his mother on at least some occasions without her batting the proverbial eyelash, but one day it happened in the presence of grandma, who was shocked and aghast. That became the occasion to draw some lines for the boy, saying, "It's all right at home, dear, especially in your own room, but please, not in front of grandma."

Most of us would like it not in front of anyone, and certainly not in public places where the law deals very swiftly with private acts engaged in publicly.

In changing the views of our time and holding up sexual intercourse as sign and seal of commitment in marriage, we have an opportunity to talk with our young people— and each other—about all the other forms of sexual expression that are short of intercourse.

We may not greatly desire heavy petting and private fondling for our children in their relations with people of the opposite sex, but if we make a strong case to reserve intercourse, then we are obliged to think about all the other expressions of sexuality. We need to work through with our young people the ages and stages at which some of these expressions might be appropriate, and how you hold them at those levels. It's an unexplored field. It will demand a high moral concern, and a great human and spiritual compassion.

Jesus' definition of adultery as looking at a woman lustfully means most men are adulterers already (Matt. 5:27-28). It also means that for the married person, any overt form of sexual exploration—even far short of intercourse—is, in fact, adultery if it is engaged in with someone who is not one's husband or wife. Thus it helps very little to have "not gone to bed" or not "gone all the way." In such cases, the "intention" was there to share physical sexual intimacy with another person in violation of one's vow of devotion and love to one's partner. Such acts indicate a serious breakdown has already come in the relation of the married partners.

Yet holding hands and kissing may be the most innocent and ingenuous expression of affection between two teenagers. And the kissing and holding of each other, and even fondling of each other, may be perfectly appropriate—if risky and dangerous—between a couple deeply in love and engaged to marry.

Yet for all our exposing of sexuality in films and magazines, our society offers few guidelines about the stages of sexual expression for different kinds of relationships. Even the Puritans of New England were far ahead of us 20th-century parents. Their practice of "bundling" was to put a young couple in love to bed with each other in a private room, but with a board down the length of the bed, between them. "It's OK to talk, to touch, to feel, but no more. There is a line." We could do well to emulate their healthy acknowledgment of the realities—both as parents and as partners and friends to each other.

There are ways to recover a sense of order and of morality and of appropriate uses of this strange thing called sex, with which we all struggle, in one way or another.

SIX

Where Teens Fit in the Sexual Cycle

All of us know the deep inner power of "doing what comes naturally." We all know what happens in the body when we are 12 to 14 years of age, and we begin to become sexual beings in a new and more mature way. Puberty produces more than hair and pimples. It produces deep longings in the loins—and in the very soul—to be united in intimacy with another human being. And the years of adolescence are spent agonizing over and sifting through all the many questions—mostly unspoken—of who and what kind of person we want that other human being to be.

Those are the years when we start literally feeling our way, and looking them over—those strange creatures of the opposite sex who seem so mysterious to us (and will, in fact, remain mysterious to us as long as we live!). This is when we are sorting out who we are and who we want that other special person to be. The problem is that no young person of 13 or 14, in this complicated, fast-moving, ever-changing, future-shock world, is likely to come to any lifetime terms with who she or he is. And it is still more difficult to match up on a lifetime basis with another of the opposite sex in a permanent partnership leading to mutual fulfillment and a positive contribution to the world.

If sexual intercourse is, in fact, the symbol and sign of the committed life of two people to each other, of two people longing to care for each other and stand by each other forever, then sexual intercourse seems to be an inappropriate sexual act for two young people in their teenage years. Other sexual acts of exploration and even of some satisfaction may be appropriate to young people awakening in spirit and body and wanting to know themselves. But sexual intercourse—if it is uniquely and intimately tied physically and philosophically to marriage—may well be out of bounds to young people who are neither ready nor able to make a permanent commitment to each other.

That's bad news to kids who feel they have received signals from the adult world that sex for them is OK—at least as long as they are quiet about it, and don't make their parents discuss what it is and what it's for, and how they should use it, if at all.

Initiating the Discussion

When I talk with ninth-grade confirmation classes about sexuality and marriage, there is a fair amount of looking at the floor and scuffling of feet and hanging of heads. But invariably that is the one class in all the year when kids rush home and tell their parents, ''We talked about sex in class today.'' Parents often report it was the stimulus for the best discussion of sex and marriage they'd ever had

with their youngsters. These parents are grateful somebody brought the subject up. They want discussion about
sex to be open and above board for their young people.

My guess is that the kids want it, too. Most of them
have had virtually no guidance at all about sexuality.
They've seen a lot and heard a lot through television and
films, but face-to-face conversation about sex with the
adults who mean the most to them and whose values they
most respect and will one day emulate is often missing. I
am convinced that they want to hear from their folks and
from their faith about sex. Because they haven't, they have
taken the silence as approval, and so they have gone farther and farther in their experimentation.

When Mary came to see me, ostensibly about her faith,
she soon moved the subject to sex. What did I think? What
is my real position? How far did I think kids should go in
sex? How do you stop if you want to stop? What do you
do if boys won't have anything to do with you if you won't
let them "score" sexually?

As we talked, she acknowledged that many of her
friends were beginning to have some kind of sexual relations with boys. She was equally clear that she wanted
to keep some standard of sexuality for herself. She even
said that she wanted to be a virgin on the day she married.
But how? That was her question.

Ellen Goodman has suggested that perhaps 17 or 18 is
old enough. She reported a list of all the "ifs" that might
make such a sexual relationship OK. The question of concerned professionals, who have almost nothing vested in
defending "traditional" morals, is, How can even 17- or
18-year-olds fulfill the "ifs" of a sexual relationship? How
can they know they won't be hurting someone, or taking
unfair advantage of each other, or falling prey to all the
"using" of other people about which feminism is so rightly

concerned? Can any young person enter into such intimacy and have it mean anything but a temporary relationship or experimentation, using another person with little intention of permanent moral and psychological—much less economic—support of the other person?

If one values permanence in relationships and honors another's deep needs and hopes and dreams, and if one wishes to respect the true person and spirit of the other, there can hardly be any circumstance that justifies sexual intercourse for two young people who are not married to each other—especially if they cherish any hopes of someday being married to another person and carrying out that relationship with honor and dignity.

Marriage and its meaning become the test for all other sexual relationships—especially those of teenagers, who are still essentially exploring life and themselves. The question for us all is, What do you want marriage to mean? What are your hopes for that relationship? How can you prepare yourself and your life for that most taxing and exciting and wonderful of all human relationships? Is there anything you can do now to be better prepared for that life of partnership? Is there anything to be thought about, planned for, and worked through that might make you a better wife or husband someday?

Most of us do have a dream for and an ideal of marriage. And for most of us, this is important enough to warrant sober thought and study and time, in the years of preparing and waiting for it.

What if our sexual philosophy and activity and attitude before marriage—beginning even in very young teenage years—has a bearing on what will happen in a future marriage? What if our cavalier attitude and demeaning of the sexual act, have, in fact, undercut and deeply hurt the future marriages for which we all cherish such hopes? If

they have—as I believe is the case—then we have a powerful reason for exercising caution and concern about how
sexuality is expressed and worked out for teenagers.

Stages of Sexual Expression

There are other levels of sexual awakening and awareness besides intercourse on which we could concentrate,
particularly in relation to the delicate matter of growing,
groping, uninformed, highly stimulated teenagers and
their sexual understanding and experience.

Why does sex for teenagers have to be a matter of "going
all the way," that is, going all the way to the level of
awesome consequences and responsibility that are a chal-
lenge even to the most mature adult? Why should growing
children have anything to do with something that may
make them suddenly parents and partners in living and
loving together in a strange and complicated world?

We glibly talk about the right of teenagers to be "sexually active" and argue about "squeal rules" that might
tell on them to their parents if they are receiving birth-
control information, but we are unwilling—or more ac-
curately, *frightened*—to deal with the real issues of what
is appropriate sexual expression at all for our teenagers.
We're embarrassed to talk seriously about other alternatives, while we look the other way to avoid seeing their
involvement in the much more serious business of intercourse, with its lifetime effects on their lives.

The struggle still is one of values. What do we want our
children to care about, to stand for, to represent in the
world? What kinds of lives do we want them to live? What
freedom do we want them to have for real choices in the
world?

Why not talk with our kids about our values? This may
mean we'll need to do a lot more thinking about what

those values really are. And we need to ask ourselves what we really want our kids to be about and to stand for.

Maybe sex in American society doesn't have to be the whole thing, replete with sexual intercourse, the crowning glory and fulfillment of all sexual longing.

What, after all, is wrong with a few years of preparation and anticipation? Some things are better when they've been prepared for, anticipated, thought about, and planned for. So why not stages of sexual expression for all of us, and not just for our teenagers?

We have allowed masturbation to be seen as a dark and evil reality in our lives—something sex researchers insist a large segment of the population, male and female, young and old, practice, and yet something we fear to acknowledge. Yet it could be a stage in experience on the way to full sexual experience. If accepted and allowed and even welcomed, it might well take a great deal of the pressure off the drive to push toward intercourse at a young age.

Children do accept other limitations from us. Psychologists tell us they even long for limitations. Saying no can be a way to grow, and saying no to intercourse may give time for the growth and maturation that may make for a new kind of stable, value-oriented, serious, and yet joyful marriage that has a chance of succeeding.

Fashioning a Sexual Ethic

What could young teenagers do to understand their sexuality and to fashion a way of living that could make them glad to be who they are, not ashamed and not afraid of their own sexuality? Here are some guidelines for them.

1. *Find someone who loves you and is interested in your life and talk with him or her about sex and what it means.* Try your minister, if you have one, and your father and mother, or a respected teacher. Say, "I respect you a lot and

know you care about me. I want to know about sex, and I've come to ask you to tell me what you know. What's good about it, and what's bad about it? Is it for everybody or just for some? How can I prepare now for a great sex life later?''

2. *Get someone who's had a long marriage and seems to be happy in it to tell you what marriage is like.* "Give me the facts," you might say. "What were the problems? How did you deal with them? Is sex fun? Is it boring after 25 years, or is it better? What does it mean to you? And what does it mean to your spouse?''

3. *Make your own love plan for your life and write down your philosophy of sex as you think it through.* Start with a picture of what you'd like your sexual life in marriage to be like, if you've decided that you want to be married someday.

4. *Think about virginity.* Is it a virtue? Is there value in preserving it? Is it a gift to offer a husband or wife someday?

5. *Work back from marriage to your present age.* If you see the goal, how do you get there? When would you like to be married? At what age? If that leaves you without a sexual partner for 10 to 15 years, how can you manage it?

6. *Make a list of how far you would go sexually,* short of intercourse, and with whom.

7. *Make a list of what else you want in your life* that would be important and fulfilling, and that would use your energy and time:

- Books to read (including books about marriage and sex, and certainly books about life, and lives, and history and people);
- Sports to play;
- Friends to make;
- Possible achievements in life;
- Clubs and activities that would be fun and fulfilling.

8. *Think about other kinds of friendships* with the opposite sex and with your own, and what you'd like them to be like.

9. *Write out a philosophy of life* and put down ideas for living it.

10. *Get involved, especially in service to others*—through church, school, and other organizations. Care about others—a wonderful goal for life.

Marriage and what you want it to be is a key to how we look at sex for teenagers. Marriage as an ideal, with intercourse seen as the heart of it, may help teenagers accept limitations before marriage.

Sex for teenagers? Yes. There can be an openness to explore themselves, to understand and begin to feel some of the pleasures God gave to the body—in a private, personal, and appropriately single way. And with others there can be the beginnings of touch, the joy of a hand held out in affection, the embrace of caring and deepening friendship. These are beginnings—just as scholastic, athletic, economic, and emotional life is at a beginning stage for young persons in their teenage years.

SEVEN

Selling Short or Gaining Long

In America, most discussion of the sexual issues has been about sex in general, as an experience we all share. It has taken little cognizance of any purpose for sex, and therefore has had little to say about its meaning. This has been the great loss for teenagers struggling with sex, and for the mid-lifers, too, also struggling with sex. Saddest of all has been a whole generation of young people entering marriage thinking that they know everything about sex, but in fact knowing almost nothing about its meaning.

It is in the meaning that the sexual experience can work wonders in long life, in deepening commitment, in permanence of relationship, in healing of the heart, and in the qualities of joy and hope in human life.

If its meaning is in drawing a man and a woman together in expressing physically their love for each other as the truest physical sign of sharing their hearts with each other, then sexual expression—culminating in sexual intercourse—is one of the most important human experiences. Next to the ecstasy of communication with God in prayer and worship, it may be the highest form of human communication given to us.

The Bible views sex as God's gift to his children. God gave woman and man to each other. God intended them to rejoice in each other. God meant them to help each other, be companions of each other, serve each other, love each other, and, incidentally, to recreate themselves—through children to populate the earth.

In the creation story and in Jesus' much later interpretation of the creation story, man and woman were meant to be husband and wife, partners in the most intimate sense, creators of humankind, but also rejoicers in each other and in the sheer joys of being alive. That meant eating together, talking together, making plans together, and eventually being parents together. Can you imagine what it must have been like to be parents of Cain and Abel, to have to deal with murder in your own household—that primeval enmity of one human being against another for jealousy and envy's sake?

Of course, Adam and Eve had already been introduced to that awful human struggle as they had dealt with their own human desires for knowledge and power and the temptation to play God by eating of the forbidden tree of the knowledge of good and evil. Suddenly they made the human discovery of their own sin, as they forsook innocence and chose selfishness and power, and learned in sorrow of their own fallibility, their own nakedness, spiritual as well as physical.

So the struggle was there, part of the human condition—the struggle with self, with desire, with ego, with power, with wanting to be first, with wanting to be recognized, acknowledged, given place by others, and most of all—the struggle to be loved. That, more than anything, is our deepest longing. "Love me, love me, love me!" is our human cry.

God gave man and woman to each other to meet that need. He gave himself in Jesus to all humankind to meet the same need, to say *love* to the human race, to say *grace* and *peace* to us in our turmoil and our struggle and our sinful separation from each other—whether in the willful misunderstanding between nations, or a three-day silence between a husband and wife over a misunderstanding.

God is with us for reconciliation. God came into the world in Jesus for reconciliation, to help people wake up to each other, forgive each other, start over again, be nice to each other again, and find joy in each other again.

Unreconciled, we are all miserable. Nothing goes right. If our relationship is not right with our fathers and our mothers, no other relationship is right. If the relationships of husbands and wives with each other are not right, they are likely to be disastrous for their children. Ultimately, none of our human relationships can be right unless our fundamental, basic relationship with God is right.

In that relationship we discover that we are not God. We don't even have to pretend to be God. So we don't have to lord it over anybody. We don't have to push other people around. We don't have to be power hungry. We don't have to be angry. We don't have to be arrogant. We don't have to put anybody down, because we are simply children of God ourselves. We are dependent ourselves. We are weak and heavy-laden ourselves. We are in need ourselves. So humility is possible. A certain measure of grace is possible. A capacity for kindness is possible. We are enabled to love people, rejoice in people, care about people, and extend ourselves on behalf of people, but most of all with one other person who is our own, our beloved, our partner.

There the whole human condition is played out and symbolized. To be ecstatic, and intimate, and sexually giving to everyone around us would be impossible, because the meanings and the self-givings would be too much, too heavy, with too many mixed messages, and with more promises and intimations than we could ever fulfill. It would therefore be destructive.

The Crucial Role of Marriage and Family

So in marriage God gives us one person with whom to symbolize and center and concentrate all that love and tenderness and yearning for intimacy that we feel. For in that one recognized, honored, legal, and committed relationship, the very deepest joys of the human experience can be shared without fear. For this is the person committed to loving you and standing by you, "for better or worse, for richer or poorer, in sickness and in health—'till death." That person loves you enough to let you have a bad day—or a bad year—and not throw you out because of it, but instead to understand, to forgive, to uphold, to care.

Two people in marriage can expect more from each other. In fact, they have rights. In Robert Frost's words, they have "promises to keep." No other human relationship comes close to that pledged relationship of trust—except the covenant agreement of people within the life of the church, where they have agreed before God to walk together as brothers and sisters in the ways of the Lord.

By its intimacy and precious commitment, marriage makes all other human relationships possible. It makes the other relationships safe and selfless and humane and helpful. It takes away the constant, predatory possibility of self-serving, lusting desires to get something for oneself in other human relationships, to "get a piece of someone," as human beings so crudely say of each other, to have part of someone else's body, to "get into" another person's body in a sexual way, to gain power over another person, to take away something from that other person, to "de-flower" that person, to take away innocence or virginity or privacy or personhood—indeed, to "rape" or steal from another what that person does not choose to give.

Marriage was intended to make all those other relationships safe from our own human, predatory, self-serving, lustful, sinful, and broken will to own other people.

Relationships have meaning and purpose, and when the meaning and purpose of marriage is fulfilled, there is a better chance for other relationships to be fulfilled. The "adulterating" of any human relationship should be less likely if the primary human relationship of marriage is right. If marriage is right, then friendship between a man and a man, a woman and a woman, a man and a woman, a woman and a man, a man or woman and a child, can be right.

Our lusts come so often from our marriages not being right. Our making victims of other people comes when we have let our marriages become selfish, or listless, or ungiving, or rigid, or angry and ill-willed. Those things happen to our marriages when our relationship with God and with our own parents is not right—and "right" means humble and honorable and respectful.

There are, after all, different things that different relationships are meant to do for us. A relationship with God is meant to help us see we are not God, to have a humble heart, to have friendship with our Creator, to know our place, to be free from arrogance. Thus the first commandment says, "I am the Lord your God . . . . You shall have no other gods before me" (Exod. 20:23).

A relationship with our parents is meant to give us someone who loves us as God loves us—unquestioningly and in spite of all we may say or do, someone who will forgive us, teach us, share the wisdom of their experience with us, and help us make it in the world. Parents are people who have been given by God a stewardship for our lives. They are to get us into life, to show us how to make it in life, and to cheer us on in life. This is a fundamental relationship we would do well not to mess up, or distort, or destroy. Thus the commandment, "Honor your father and your mother . . . that it may go well with you" (Deut. 5:16).

A relationship with one person in marriage is to help us keep some purity of heart, some innocence, some freedom in the midst of our deep human passions so we do not covet other human beings' bodies or lives. Thus, the commandments that we should not "commit adultery" and that we should not "covet your neighbor's wife . . . or anything that belongs to your neighbor" (Exod. 20:14, 17). In coveting, desiring something that isn't ours, we are likely to break the human covenant that allows us to live together in society, able to be trusted by our neighbor, and, indeed, by our own wife or husband. To adulterate a human relationship is to make it impure, to mix it up with other things, to lose its sense of purpose, to devalue it and distort it, and, in fact, to create within it a dis-ease.

Marriage makes an anchor, a touchstone for all other human relationships. It provides a safeguard for those relationships. It gives them order and place. It is the crucial and basic human relationship for society, and out of it comes the family and the community.

All people need to find ways of relating to each other, of belonging. The first place this happens is in the family. If we don't, if we are hurt, or abused, or ignored, or squelched and downtrodden there, all our other human relationships will be distorted. Even our relationship with God will be distorted.

When you read the stories of the men in our state and federal penitentiaries, you read of havoc in the home, of orphaned boys with no one to love and guide them, or of

boys hurt or beaten or abused or neglected at home—
bereft of father, bereft of love, abandoned to the world
and its demons before any defenses could be mounted.

The family is crucial to our whole system of life together
in communities where trust and obedience and loyalty are
what make life and law—and therefore safety and respect
and just plain human functioning—possible. Otherwise,
it is "every man for himself"—everyone out to do everybody else in, everyone out to rape, pillage, steal, hurt, kill,
and destroy everyone and everything else.

Order, law, cooperation, and relationship—the things
that allow a society to function—come from a basic trust,
born originally of primal love. Law itself never makes human society work. It is trust in the law to be right and
good, and trust in other people to do what is right and
good, that makes society work.

All of that comes from the commitments and promises
that we ourselves make. The commitment to another human being in marriage—given freely and with love—is
the basic commitment of all our life. It is our deepest and
highest promise, second only to the one we make to God.

If any of this is true, then marriage, and the honoring
and preservation of marriage, are critical for our whole
society's life, and for each one of our personal lives—
whether we ourselves marry or not. That institution, that
basic relationship among human beings, needs to be
understood and honored.

Many young people today dismiss marriage as a mere
piece of paper—and as meaningless to them. Living together, "as long as it's a good relationship," is all that they
think is important. "Who needs promises and paper?"
they ask. In that setting, sexual intercourse has no power
for permanence. It does not support or make possible loyalty. It is not a sign or a seal. It is no sacrament.

So to use sex—indiscriminately—is to sell short instead of to gain long. It is to forsake the long gain in order to win the short pleasure, the immediate gratification.

Sex As Sacramental

Sex is sacramental and meant for marriage, not because it is the means for procreating the race, but because it is the sign of the deepest love God has given us, the love of two people who have committed themselves to each other for life.

To be sacramental, the sexual act needs to be viewed in that way not only by those who marry, but also by those who do not marry—those who have chosen not to marry, or who have never found someone to marry, or who once were married and out of the hurt experienced in that relationship were divorced and chose a single life.

Can sex be sacramental for them, too? Can it be something they, too, recognize as having its full meaning as the heart of marriage, and therefore as something from which they would want to abstain until they should choose to marry?

Many say that's asking a lot. Many still say, "It's my business what I do. Sex is part of being an adult human being. I have a right to sex."

That's convincing until they seriously consider marriage. For most people who are deeply in love and decide to be married, there suddenly comes to be a new set of expectations and assumptions and even rules. All of a sudden you want a partner who is only yours, someone who hasn't been promiscuous, someone who may even come to life with you as a virgin—or at least with a new, high view of marriage and sex, even though he or she may have come to it after a dramatic change of heart and view.

Art came to be married as a man of 50 who had already been married for a number of years before going through a painful divorce. He was a distinguished professional man with a delicious sense of humor built on repartee, fast answers, and a basically happy heart and positive view of life.

Marnie, a divorced woman whom he dearly loved, was someone who had learned the ways of prayer, of the Spirit, and of the ministry of love. She and I were also good friends.

Art was more than a little skeptical of this minister who had become a friend of his intended and this church that had become her family. But after an initial confrontation the first day of our premarital counseling, Art and I became fast friends.

Yet there was a hitch. Before her new faith and change of heart and while she was living the single life, Marnie had fallen into a relationship with a man whom Art could not abide. This character had even lived in with Marnie in a sexual way for a number of months.

Art knew it and felt that as a modern man, freed up about all that sort of thing, he had to accept what that relationship had been and to forgive and forget. The only trouble was, he couldn't. "Everything I know about Marnie," he said a year after their marriage, "stands against and defies any possibility of that kind of relationship with a character like that. What could she ever have seen in him? At night I have dreams of Marnie living with and having sex with that man. Her married relationship years before doesn't bother me at all, but that live-in relationship with that jerk revolts me and gives me secret feelings of antipathy toward Marnie."

There are some things for which an urbane, mature, liberated view simply do not account. There are times in life when we want desperately for the one we love, especially the one we marry, to come with some semblance of purity and principle to that relationship. And that can be only if two people have held those principles and made some attempt to live by them prior to marriage.

Those memories for Art were finally healed as we prayed about them and talked them through, but Art's struggle suggests that our way of living, our principles, our ethics, make more difference to us than most of us acknowledge.

Tanya is a young woman in her late 20s, with a graduate degree, single and living in an apartment with a male student and another female student. They share expenses and housekeeping duties, but never a bed.

Tanya is a virgin and likes it that way. She has several times been in love, but nothing has yet worked out. She has seen enough of her friends' sorrows in marriage that she has little desire to be married just for the sake of being married. She clearly would like to be married someday.

Why doesn't she have sex with the single young men who are known to her? For one thing, she longs for love and believes it would be very difficult to share that intimacy with someone with whom she was not in love. Also, she has thought a lot about marriage and has somehow never grown jaded or cynical about it. She still looks forward to the possibility of such a relationship for her. The high view of marriage she has held since her early teen years has been a source of hope and expectation in her life and therefore made life without sex possible—not easy, but possible.

Charlotte, her friend, 15 years older than Tanya, has never married, but has had one affair that became a sexual relationship. During that period she drifted away from some of her earlier values, including her faith values.

As time went on, the relationship waned and the philosophy that went with it paled and seemed increasingly inadequate. She wanted to believe there was something better in life. She hadn't quite given up hope for marriage.

At 40 she came to know a man whose life had fallen in after many years of marriage and a bout with alcoholism. Though recovering from that addiction, he was still lonely. He and Charlotte found each other, fell in love, and have had an exemplary marriage.

"I am so glad I found my way back to a better way before I met Matt," she has said many times. Principles mean something.

Is this the way for all single people—divorced or never married? Perhaps not. But many whom we see in our counseling ministry are hurt because some failure "to act justly and to love mercy and to walk humbly with your God" destroyed their marriage (Mic. 6:8). The pain of divorce has given them a new view of values, of principles, of the worth in forsaking the present pleasure for the long gain.

Selling Short and Selling Out

A surprising number of singles are coming to see that "selling short" is, in fact, "selling out" something personal and precious of their inner self, their own integrity. That is what they find they are preserving by giving up sexual pleasure now, for its far greater fulfillment later, in marriage.

What of those who never marry? Those who have tried many unmarried sexual relationships confess that they are really not very happy. They still become attached to people, and breaking up is still painful.

Barbie, a divorced, middle-aged woman, came in very angry about the man who wouldn't marry her. "But I had made a commitment!" she said. What she meant was, she had given herself to him sexually. To her that was a commitment. But it was not a commitment for him. Her expectations had gone far beyond the realities. And something that she now realized was of great importance to her had been lost—her integrity, her self. She felt "had," robbed. Yet she had knowingly given it all away. "Never again," she said later.

The high view of marriage as the scene for sex has power as a goal and ideal to help people live singly without sex. It allows them to be more whole and more truly themselves, and eventually to rejoice in that integrity, or as is so often said today, "to feel good about themselves."

There is a way of the heart for single people that can be fulfilling, and hopeful, and whole. Those who have chosen it say the gain in the heart and spirit, in the self, is worth it.

Selling short is not really what anyone wants today. It is not what most folks in love would do, if they realized they were doing it. They want to gain long. They want to go for permanence. They want to be together for life.

By destroying the symbol, they have made unlikely, if not impossible, the sacrament. By their own hand, they have lost that which, with all their hearts, they wanted most to gain.

To give marriage a chance to be what it was meant to be, to let sexual intercourse stand as the sign of its intimacy and intention, is to give us back the anchor and base for a system of sexual ethics that has the chance of helping us to wholeness, hope, and joy in this gift that was meant for ecstasy and not for agony.

What then becomes critical is how we do marriage, what place we give to sex and its expression in this one vital, committed, human relationship.

EIGHT

Growing Old Together

What is needed more than a sexy marriage? A marriage in which the sexual relation is not fearful, frozen, frigid, nervous, limited, or lackadaisical, but freely loving, glad, joyful, exciting, fun, full of play, wild, free, and fulfilling in every way possible for both partners?

Our ideal of sex in marriage can be good enough to wait for. It can be exciting and free and ecstatic enough to allow stages from teenage exploration and affection through courtship's commitment and pleasuring and touching as honest and acknowledged and even appropriate levels of preparation for full sexual sharing and long progress toward it.

Sex in marriage need not be dark, mysterious, forbidden, and wicked, but can be free, rejoicing, longed for, and healthy. It can be something we never want to lose, something we'd never trade for any illicit love, something of the human spirit and the body's ecstasy that could never be matched by any affair, no matter how wickedly wonderful.

If self-pleasuring (or masturbation) for the young, the

old, the absent, and the separated can have meaning as a partial fulfillment, as promise of something to come or as memory of something that was, or as relief and release in the face of something unlikely ever to be, then it is something wonderful indeed.

As long as the affair, or the pornographic, or the massage parlor, or prostitution is allowed to appear to offer something better—better sex, a bigger orgasm, more sexy stimulation, more wide-eyed variety, more positions, more power to turn us on, then the more impossible will be the task of marriage in succeeding, in winning back its place as the highest ideal, the most sexual relationship, the most fulfilling life.

After all, those today who wish to laud the advantages of homosexual liaison have only to recite the sins of heterosexual marriage in its tawdry angers and abuses and neglects to make their case seem an almost viable alternative to marriage as we have come to know it. For marriage today is full of anger, competition, abuse, hurt, unfaithfulness, and brokenness. It is a travesty of what God meant for it. It is a misunderstood relationship, a far-too-often un-worked-on relationship. It is a relationship born of people who thought they'd make it on love and their good communication skills, on what good people they perceived themselves to be. So misguided they are, and so disillusioned they become.

One of the most beautiful women I have ever known used to come in every once in a while to pour out the story of her marriage. It was the story of a husband well-dressed, good-looking, and successful, who fell more and more into a pattern of withdrawal, of absence, and eventually going to prostitutes for sex. He and his hunting buddies had hired two prostitutes to go with them on a weekend "hunting" trip to "service" them all.

"Two prostitutes!" I gasped. I wanted to add, ". . . when he has someone as beautiful as you at home, who is his wife who loves him?" It was too bizarre. I simply could not understand it.

Clearly, it is not physical beauty and outward appearance on which marriages are built. Great sex can never, by itself, make or break a marriage. It is in the heart, in the spirit, that marriages are made. It is the way we see each other and the way we see ourselves that makes a marriage.

Jerry loathed himself. So much anger had lived in his home as a child. A physical blemish had scarred his body and his soul. It symbolized outside a mark he had felt inside, an inadequacy, a self-hatred, a fear of never being loved that had apparently haunted him since he was a child. He never believed that his beautiful wife loved him, though she did so deeply.

That Jerry and Cappie had lived together for 15 years, had raised two beautiful children, and had once been very happy together, says to me that there must have been a way. The demise of that marriage didn't have to have come. I cannot believe those two beautiful people could not somehow have grown old together.

Every couple I have ever married wanted to grow old together. "Come, grow old with me!"—Robert Browning's classic and beloved invitation to Elizabeth Barrett— is the winsome summation of exactly what they wanted for their life together: the chance to grow old as partners; the chance to mature through the years into ripe friendship and deep, instinctive understanding; the chance to share hurts and hopes, terrible tragedy and times of triumph together, and grow through them to deeper love and deeper unity.

Every couple I know has wanted to think they could stick by each other despite baldness and wrinkles, over-weight and bad habits. By confession and forgiveness, mutual help and healing, they hoped for a life together lifted from plodding partnership into the realm of exhilarating adventure.

Every couple agrees with that when I bring it up. None of them wants a short-term marriage. All of them think they have what it takes to succeed in a lifetime together. They look at each other knowingly, as if they have a secret I couldn't possibly know that guarantees them long life together, a fulfilled, happy life.

They have common interests. They like each other. "We were friends first, and later lovers," they often say. "We communicate well. We always say exactly what we feel, what may be bothering us about the other. And we always work it out." Good communication, I suspect, is what they feel will guarantee this marriage's success.

Why, then, does it so rarely happen? Why, then, does first blush so often become pale pallor on a bloom long gone? Why does excitement turn to tedium, and fascination and fun become boredom and antipathy? Why do perfectly fine people, who really are in love, so quickly begin to take each other for granted and put their whole marriage at risk?

I have married so many middle-aged couples who, after divorces or deaths, come together to make the marriage of the century, acting together like adolescents in love, so attentive to each other, so full of grace toward each other, always smiling, always acting on behalf of the other, so happy. Yet within months they are back to being like so many other married people, with the light gone from the eye, the hand no longer held, the touching and the silly grin so sadly absent.

Signs of Love

A lovely, winsome, middle-aged wife of a corporate executive once said to me with a far-off look in her eye, "Oh,
I do wish George would just once in a while hold my
hand, or put his arm around me—in public!" Probably he
does it in private, at least in the bedroom. But what she
wanted was in public, out where the world would know
he was her man and she was his woman. She wanted to
be reassured, before witnesses, that her husband loved her,
was not ashamed of her, and did not think of her merely
as an appendage to his busy business life.

How human, and, I think, how true of all human life
her statement was. None of us wants to be taken for granted. All of us hunger for signs of affection.

Little do most of us know the sensation of thrill and
chill that can run through our bodies at the merest touch
of the hand of the one we love, on an arm or a leg, or
from an arm thrown lightly over the shoulder by a dear
one in an unexpected, if not public, place. We don't know
because it has been so long since we did it ourselves, or
had it done to us.

Why? I often ask myself as I look at so many marriages.
Why do we insist on taking each other so for granted?
Why do we think we will always have our partner? Do
we think there automatically will be a better one, a more
loving or beautiful one, a sexier one out there for us to
find?

Why do we not touch more, look at each other more
often and more lovingly, hold hands more consciously,
say loving, complimentary things more often, pat each
other more daringly in the intimate places of the body
when least expected and just to signal to our beloved—
even out in public—that wonderful sense of the shared
secret of our intimacy and our love?

If you think the Bible is staid and stuffy, read the Song of Solomon, that beautiful, earthy, and intimate expression of physical love! Is it all analogy, all a sign of God and Israel? I think not. I think God, who created us, yearns for us to remember we were sent to love. "A new commandment I give you," said Jesus. "Love one another" (John 13:34).

Serving One Another in Love

I have the feeling that many, many of us are afraid, afraid of each other, afraid of revealing to another that self we know we are. In a surprising number of our marriages I believe an unspoken cover-up is going on.

John and Betty came to see me separately. They were in their middle 40s. They loved one another, but they each told the same story.

"Betty wouldn't understand me if she knew what I really want in life. If she knew my fantasies and desires, I'm afraid she'd leave me. Certainly, she'd think less of me, probably lose her respect for me. I can't tell her who I am inside, and yet I don't want to go on not being known by the person I love so much. I'm not ready to take the risk of telling her."

"John is so quiet and reserved," Betty said. "I can't tell what he thinks. He's good-looking, and a wonderful guy, and I love him dearly. But in some ways he's, well, dull. He seems afraid to take chances. I want to cut loose, be free, take some chances—even in our personal lives, even in our sexual life. But John is so much the quiet, steady type that even my saying it would just blow him away. I don't want to hurt him, but I also don't want to go on for another 20 years together like this."

They were afraid to risk with each other—but what a surprise when finally they did! It was a happy surprise that proved a breakthrough and the salvation of their marriage.

In the right context, in the relationship of marriage, I believe God gave us sex to be our joy, our delight, something beautiful and ecstatic, beyond the power of any erotic novel or pornographic film or prostitute's scanty outfit to describe or fantasize or promise. But we have lost our imaginations. We have grown weary in well-doing. We have given up trying to be beautiful, to be loving, to be sexy.

In this day of adultery, this age of predatory invasion of marriage and its commitment, if there is anything required of married people beyond their daily prayers and their faithful searching together for the living God in their life, it is their obligation to be somebody beautiful for their partner, somebody sexy for their partner, somebody well-dressed and alluring and delightful and exotic and stimulating and romantic for their partner.

If you will not do it, there is someone else out there with an eye for your woman, your man, who will do it. And you will be perceived as not having cared enough to try.

Nothing is worse than that lame defense that I hear from many middle-aged couples, "You're married to me! I don't have to lose weight, or fix my face, or clean my breath, or stop my bad habits, or be sexy, and look beautiful or handsome for you. You should love me the way I am— no requirements, no conditions, no nothing!" How different from courtship's days, when it was a constant round of knocking oneself out to be kind, attractive, fun, and beautiful for the other.

A defiant, angry spirit grows with the years, and secretly husbands and wives are at war with each other. They defy the other's desires. They tell themselves they are preserving their own personalities, their own rights by their defiance. But what they are doing is defying their own vow and promise. They are sowing the seeds of destruction and divorce in their marriage.

Scripture says we are in life to serve others, to meet their needs, to offer ourselves to them in love. Should not our marriage partner be the one beyond all others whom we would seek in every way possible to serve?

There is very little that is out of bounds in the sexual relationship of a husband and wife. That is what marriage is. As long as it is loving, almost anything goes. When it is unloving, when it is selfish, when it hurts, it has gone too far.

Why should people in love, who are married to each other, allow the eyes and the mind and maybe the heart of the other to stray to anyone or anything besides the beloved partner—to the erotic film or the pornographic magazine, or the stripper, or the masseuse, or the neighbor, or the prostitute?

Why should not all of that be satisfied right at home? And if it can't be, then talk about it, and share as openly and honestly as you can what you will allow beyond that.

It is the notion of the indecency of sexual stimulation and play that is the enemy I believe needs to be fought in our marriages if they are to survive. Only when it is too late do we realize that from the beginning we are fighting for survival. Loyalty and love are being ever tested, always at stake.

Should they be at stake? No, but the world we live in is too much. We are in competition for everything, and most of all we are in competition for our wives, and our husbands. By taking them for granted, we may lose them.

Three out of five lose them today—an absolutely stagger-
ing and terrifying statistic—and a shame and an embar-
rassment to the Christians who are presumably most committed to loving, to forgiveness, to serving others, to going
to the end of the world for another—as Jesus did.

Nurturing the Heart

While attention to the sexual is critical, the final issue
is told by the heart. It is the heart, most of all, that needs
nurturing, and that nurturing comes by faith.

The real excitement of sex is in the mind, in our perception of the other. It is in attitude and feeling about
another human being. It is the absence of feeling that is
most often given as the first justification for divorce: "I
don't feel anything for him or her anymore. I just don't
love him."

Those changes in feeling and perception have come, I
think, from an inattention to God in marriage, to not having taken seriously enough how critical it is to hold the
physical and the spiritual together, to love God together,
if you want to still be loving each other and living happily
together 50 years down the line.

Loving God gives a perspective to life. If, as the Bible
says, "God is love," then any institution built on love had
better be in constant touch with the one who is the source
of love—the one who creates it, renews it, restores it, and
gives it back again and again.

When Ginny and Bob came to talk about getting married, they'd never been to church. A girlfriend at work
had told Ginny about her wedding at our church and had
commended us. They weren't particularly for or against
Christ and his church. It simply hadn't occurred to them.
All they knew was that they wanted to be married and

that a church building like ours would certainly be a pretty setting for their wedding.

I made it clear that the faith is what we were about and what our whole process of preparation for marriage was about. We talked about faith, about Jesus and his love, about prayer and the Bible, and believing, and worship, and particularly about forgiving and healing hurts. All of a sudden, faith in a marriage began to make some sense to them. Who was going to help them forgive when they didn't· want to forgive? They hadn't thought about that. That God could do that, and wanted to do that, and loved them enough to do that for them was an intriguing idea.

"We'll try it," Bob said.

"How about coming to church tomorrow, for starters," I asked, hardly daring.

"OK," Ginny said, "I'd like that."

They came and have never stopped coming. They've joined a breakfast Bible study group. They're praying together at home.

Three years later they said, "We never would have made it through the first year without prayer and without God. And you know what? The sex has been a lot better, too."

There is a connection. Love is crucial for sex, and God gives love.

Growing Old Together

Two people in marriage grow old together, grow riper and richer and more deeply in love, not just because they have wept and suffered together, but because they have taken risks with each other. They have swallowed their pride. They have probed and learned. They have discovered deep secrets—of weaknesses, of sorrows, of fears, of lonelinesses, of dreams and hopes, of sins and sicknesses, of fetishes and failures.

They have learned to live with them all. They haven't always liked them. They haven't always liked everything about each other. They have surely had to forgive much. But they have adjusted, accepted, and learned to like new things and give up old things. Most of all, they have learned to take chances with each other, to trust each other with secrets and with sins, to dare to share a truth and still have hope.

They have grown. Their capacity has enlarged. Chances are, they've come to be proud of each other, supportive of each other, admiring of each other. They've learned ways to not take each other for granted. They have realized that this world is just as predatory and full of risk for them and their marriage as it is for their children just starting out, and that they'd jolly well better be working at their marriage.

There is probably no way to keep sex from being a struggle—among the best of people and in the best of marriages. But when it is seen and accepted as a sacred gift from the Creator, given to be enjoyed, for the fulfilling of relationship, and the increasing of love, then it becomes a wonderful anchor, a great goal, a sign for measuring life.

Not everyone will have it—and there is always sorrow in that. Even those who do will not always fulfill it. But for us all, the right kind of sex, accepted as gift, centered in marriage, becomes a hope and a memory that can add expectation and reflection, some measure of acceptance and fulfillment, and maybe peace—for all of us who are trying, who accept with joy any part of this great gift from God that may, by his grace, come to us.